The Seven Core Issues in Adoption and Permanency Workbook for Children and Teens *also by the author*

Seven Core Issues in Adoption and Permanency
A Comprehensive Guide to Promoting Understanding and Healing
Allison Davis Maxon and Sharon Kaplan Roszia
Foreword by Deborah N. Silverstein, MSW
ISBN 978 1 78592 823 9
eISBN 978 1 78450 930 9

The Seven Core Issues Workbook for Parents of Traumatized Children and Teens
A Guide to Help You Explore Feelings and Overcome Emotional Challenges in Your Family
Allison Davis Maxon and Sharon Kaplan Roszia
Illustrated by Liza Stevens
ISBN 978 1 78775 669 4
eISBN 978 1 7877 567 0

The Seven Core Issues in Adoption and Permanency Workbook for Children and Teens

A Trauma-Informed Resource

ALLISON DAVIS MAXON

Illustrated by Liza Stevens

Jessica Kingsley Publishers
London and Philadelphia

First published in Great Britain in 2023 by Jessica Kingsley Publishers
An imprint of John Murray Press

1

A CIP catalogue record for this title is available from the British Library and the Library of Congress

ISBN 9 781 83997 576 9
eISBN 9 781 83997 577 6

Printed and bound in the United States by Integrated Books International

Jessica Kingsley Publishers' policy is to use papers that are natural, renewable and recyclable products and made from wood grown in sustainable forests. The logging and manufacturing processes are expected to conform to the environmental regulations of the country of origin.

Jessica Kingsley Publishers
Carmelite House
50 Victoria Embankment
London EC4Y 0DZ

www.jkp.com

John Murray Press
Part of Hodder & Stoughton Limited
An Hachette UK Company

This workbook is dedicated to children and teens who have experienced foster care, kinship and adoption. May the Force be with YOU, always!

Dear Parents and Caregivers,

Thank you for loving and supporting your child and teen as they continue on their journey of growth and healing. This workbook has been built as a guide to help children and teens identify, explore and understand some of the complex challenges and feelings connected to adoption, foster care and kinship.

For over 30 years, I have been working directly with children, teens and adults who have experienced foster care, kinship and adoption. Their stories, pain, suffering, strength and resilience have been imprinted on my soul. Every part of the teachings in this book has been informed by the innate wisdom that survivors of trauma and traumatic losses carry within themselves.

If you are a parent who is struggling to understand and connect to your child, please read *The Seven Core Issues Workbook for Parents of Traumatized Children and Teens* by Allison Davis Maxon and Sharon Kaplan Roszia. Being in the #traumatrenches is no easy task! Parents need specific attachment skills and emotional regulation knowledge to help support the growth and healing of their child.

Please have empathy and compassion for yourself. Find other parents who are in the #traumatrenches who can support YOUR growth and learning process.

This workbook will serve as a guide to help your child or teen understand their past, claim their story, identify losses and challenges, and build on their strengths and identity. Your task is to support their journey of growth and healing.

Warm regards, Allison

FOR PROFESSIONALS AND PARENTS USING THE WORKBOOK

We cannot heal what we cannot acknowledge!

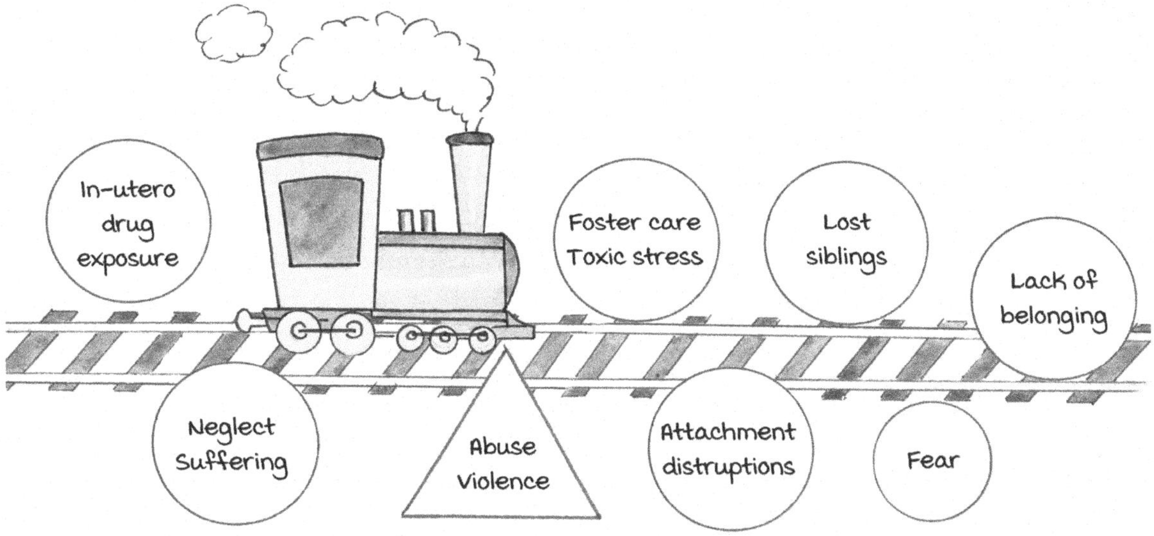

Our understanding of the *Seven Core Issues, Attachment and Trauma* enables us to better address the complex challenges and feelings that children and teens experience through various stages of their development. This workbook provides a roadmap to help children and teens explore the complexities built into adoption and permanency through skill-building activities and exercises. It is designed intentionally to be strengths-based and empowering for children and teens. Learning the emotional skills to overcome one of life's most intense and traumatic losses is no easy task. Professionals and parents can use the workbook to support and guide children and teens through a process of exploring, understanding and healing. It has been constructed to be utilized in a scaffolded process, where one activity builds to the next. I encourage parents and professionals to take their time and allow children and teens to guide their own journey through the Seven Core Issues. The workbook will help children and teens explore, process, think, feel and express themselves as they move through the various tools and activities.

All children, including those placed at birth, experience attachment disruptions—the severing of the attachments from their parents and families of origin. The child/teen/adult will be understanding and processing this major life-altering event through each developmental stage of their life. A child's developmental understanding of adoption and permanency changes and unfolds over time, as their ability to understand what adoption and permanency is generally (why some children are not raised by their birth/first parents), and what happened to them specifically (why they are not living with their birth/first parents) evolves. Babies, children and teens experience the traumatic losses associated with losing their connections to their birth/first families through a series of unfolding insights and understandings that often trigger the deep feelings, challenges and additional developmental tasks associated with the Seven Core Issues. I encourage professionals and parents to read *Seven Core Issues in Adoption and Permanency: A Comprehensive Guide to Promoting Understanding and Healing in Adoption, Foster Care, Kinship Families and Third-Party Reproduction* by Sharon Kaplan Roszia and Allison Davis Maxon.

One of the most profound losses any human can experience is the loss of their parents. Babies and children who are displaced from their birth/first parents may also lose an entire familial tree, including the ancestry, history and lineage from that tree. Some children may lose their culture, ethnic/racial identity, language and country of origin. The separations may have occurred at a pre-verbal stage of development when the child had no way of understanding or giving language to the overwhelming trauma, losses and feelings associated with what they were experiencing. The neuroscience research has shifted the focus to the vulnerable and malleable brain of the infant/child, who is often moved several times before attachment permanency is gained. This creates toxic stress that impacts brain development. Children enter foster care due to neglect, physical abuse, sexual abuse, domestic violence and in-utero drug exposure, and many will suffer the ongoing effects of complex developmental trauma. The child/teen's body may be loaded with toxic stress, fear and anxiety, easily triggered into distressed states of internal disorganization, shame and self-loathing. They may have sensory integration challenges and struggle to find internal calmness, organization and regulation. It's important to note that the mind lives in the body. If the body cannot relax, the mind has trouble focusing, learning and retaining information.

Parenting a child who fears the emotional intimacy of parent-child attachment may be a new challenge for many parents. The child who has learned to fear attachment and emotional closeness may be aggressive, moody, fearful, defiant, oppositional, numb, angry, disrespectful, anxious and controlling. When a little body cannot relax, even things like falling asleep, enjoying a meal, playing with your sibling, reading a book or following directions become challenging for both child and parent.

The majority of people in our culture were not raised in a family where adoption, foster care or kinship care were the norm. Few people imagine that they will be infertile, lose a child or grow up in another family. People generally have a vision for how they think their life will unfold. This does not occur for those individuals and families touched by foster/kinship care or adoption. There are additional developmental tasks that parents will be helping their children achieve and master. Parents are encouraged to help their child explore their strengths, challenges, thoughts and feelings through a series of exercises, activities and skill-building tools.

It's important to know that parents have their own unique journey of losses and emotional challenges when parenting through foster/kinship care and adoption. I recommend parents explore their own attachment and loss history by doing the activities and exercises in *The Seven Core Issues Workbook for Parents of Traumatized Children and Teens* by Allison Davis Maxon and Sharon Kaplan Roszia. The resources, activities and practice tools will strengthen a parent's ability to effectively address their child's trauma history, attachment impairments and core issues.

This workbook was designed to help children and teens understand their body, heart and mind, to empower them to understand and know that their story belongs to them. Where facts flounder, fantasies flourish. When children don't know the truth or facts of their story, they often fill in the blanks with 'made-up stories', sometimes scary or hurtful stories like 'I think I was a bad or unloveable baby'. It's important to note that we are all storytellers, narrating our own life journey. Children are developing their own narrative and story about their life, what happened to them and why. Their early trauma, losses and attachment disruptions can easily assist them in becoming a very negative storyteller as they narrate their own life story inside their body, heart and mind. Many children and teens find it difficult to talk about the hurtful and painful experiences and feelings connected to their loss history and trauma. Feelings of abandonment, rejection, shame and grief can intensify in the teen years as identity building becomes a central theme. In this book, all of these complex issues and challenges are explored in a strengths-based way, empowering the child and teen to more deeply understand themselves and learn effective ways to express what is in their body, heart and mind.

Please note that the activities in this workbook are downloadable by visiting the website https://library.jkp.com/redeem and using the code UYZNCNH.

FOUNDATIONAL VALUES OF THIS WORKBOOK

Grief, loss and trauma must be acknowledged.

Parenting any child can be an emotionally draining experience. Children with trauma, loss and grief need parents who can be emotionally available and responsive to their distress, hurt, fear, terror, anger and pain. The ability to emotionally regulate and emotionally attune to their child's deepest wounds and suffering is an additional task for foster, kinship and adoptive parents.

Adults need to make changes too.

Children should not be expected to make all the changes when they come into a new home. Grown-ups must make changes too. It is important that children see adults trying to change, grow and learn as well. Permanency requires adaptation for all members of the family. All little humans need and deserve unconditional love and commitment from their grown-ups!

Adoption and permanency is a lifelong, intergenerational process that brings both grief and joy to individuals and families.

Adoption and permanency is a lifelong process that is not complete when the adoption or legal process is finalized. There can be feelings of great joy as well as great loss throughout the various developmental stages of both the child and family.

Children's losses must be reduced whenever possible.

Adoption and permanency begins with loss. Without loss, adoption and permanency would not occur. All those involved in the process experience loss and grief. The way those losses are resolved will impact children throughout their lives. Our goal is to ensure that the greater burden of loss is carried by the adults rather than by the children. The task for parents is to help their child know and understand their story from the beginning, which is where the losses and/or trauma reside. This allows the child to grieve incrementally as they understand their story with more and more detail as they grow and mature. The workbook will guide parents through a process so they can help their child explore and understand the complex thoughts and feelings that are created by the experience of foster care, kinship and adoption. Many children and teens feel overwhelmed and isolated with the deep feelings connected to their core losses. Empowering parents to emotionally attune with their child's grief process can lessen their feelings of isolation. Sorrow shared is halved, while joy shared is doubled!

Families are the healing mechanism of the child.

It is the parent's task to heal a child. A therapist can help, but it is not the therapist's job to heal the child. Parents need to learn as much as possible about creating and sustaining a safe, loving and healing relationship with their child or teen. It is the primary attachment relationship between the parent and child that is the 'healing mechanism'. Parents should not be sitting in the waiting room while a therapist takes their child into an office for an hour. Families need to be included in the therapeutic process. Healing takes place 24 hours a day, seven days a week, not one hour a week in the therapist's office.

Birth/first families matter.

It is important to talk about birth/first families with children, helping them make or keep appropriate connections between themselves and their birth/first families. Appropriate information needs to be available for children to develop a sense of who they are, where they came from, why they were adopted/placed and who they will become. This workbook will give specific guidance as to how to help children and teens understand their story and acknowledge all of the difficult and complex feelings connected to their foster, kinship or adoption journey.

There are additional tasks for adoptive, foster and kinship parents.

All of us have 'legal parents', 'genetic parents' and 'parenting parents'. Most of us were raised in families where all of those roles were filled by the same parents. For children who have multiple sets of parents in these various roles, it can feel confusing and overwhelming at different stages of their development. A child may have birth/first parents, foster parents, kinship parents and adoptive parents, all of whom are 'real' and important to them. Understanding 'what happened?', 'why it happened' and 'when it happened' is an important developmental task for children who are not being raised by their birth/first parents.

Honor and respect diversity, including sexual orientation, race, culture, ethnicity, religion, gender and age.

All individuals and families have a culture, ethnicity and race. As children move from one family to another, they always experience a change of culture. These changes may also include race, ethnicity, socio-economic differences and spiritual practices. As we move children from one family tree to another, cultural, ethnic and racial identities can be lost, merged, forgotten, assimilated or honored. Ongoing open relationships with the birth/first family benefits children; openness can help address the various cultural, racial and ethnic identity challenges the baby/child/teen must navigate. Children should not have to lose any part of their identity in order to gain the stability of a family.

Professionals need to be clinically competent in attachment, trauma and adoption/permanency issues.

It is not enough to be a trained therapist or social worker when working in adoption and permanency. Specialized training in attachment, trauma and adverse childhood experiences, as well as the unique dynamics of foster care, kinship and adoption-built families, is vital. We would hope that all professionals are educated about the Seven Core Issues in adoption and permanency and are using the practices and interventions outlined in all three books to address these issues with children, adults and families. Current mental health practices that do not offer stable, consistent and skilled therapists in these areas do more of a disservice as they create more losses and reinforce already fragile attachment skills for the child/family. Our inadequate and limited mental health diagnostic categories often lead professionals to misdiagnose and hence mistreat and often medicate inappropriately.

Success means the child has a family for life.

Success is defined as a child gaining a permanent family. It is not defined as a perfect child within a perfect family. It is not defined as a child achieving success to make his or her parents proud. Our goal is always to maximize the child's potential, within the reality of the child's abilities. Having a supportive family who remains committed to the child, even as mental health issues intensify, often in adolescence, is imperative. As teens work hard to do the emotional work of building an identity and an authentic self, all the questions and deep feelings connected to their traumatic losses and separation from their birth/first parents often resurface. A family that nurtures strengths, while working on areas that need healing, will help to maximize all areas of their child's potential.

— PART 1 —

CHILDREN

CONTENTS

Hello!

This book is all about YOU! YOUR life, YOUR beliefs, YOUR feelings and everything that has happened to YOU! The good stuff and the hard stuff!

It's all a part of the story of YOU!

Understanding all the different parts of YOUR life and YOUR story is really important.

YOU may have thoughts, feelings and questions about things you don't remember or were confused about because you were so little, or scared, or overwhelmed, or hurt.

This workbook was built for YOU to explore and better understand YOURSELF! Everything that happens to YOU in YOUR life becomes a part of YOUR story. Understanding and making sense of the difficult things that have happened takes a little work. That's why we call it a 'workbook'.

Because your journey and your story belong to YOU, it's best to know and understand all the different parts of YOUR life story.

Be Bold. Be Curious. Be YOU!

I AM...

Please put a tick against the things that are true for you and add any qualities we missed next to the blank lines.

☐ Funny	☐ Hungry	☐ Adventuresome
☐ Brave	☐ Energetic	☐ Confident
☐ Creative	☐ Helpful	☐ Loyal
☐ Playful	☐ Athletic	☐ Curious
☐ Silly	☐ Friendly	☐ Responsible
☐ Caring	☐ Awesome	☐ Generous
☐ Smart	☐ Kind	☐ Observant
☐	☐	☐ ....
☐	☐	☐ ....

There are many different parts to ONE AMAZING me!!

ALL KINDS OF FAMILIES

Did you know there are lots and lots of different kinds of families?

Children can be born into their families or adopted or fostered into their families. Some families have one child and others may have four, five or six children. Some families have children who were born and adopted into the family.

Some families look alike, and other families have people who look different from each other. Some families have only one mommy. Some families may have two mommies or two daddies. Sometimes a grandparent, or aunt or uncle or foster parent is taking care of a child.

All families are real, valuable and important.

GOOD BABIES!

All babies are Good Babies!

Here's a picture of me as a baby

There is no such thing as a Bad Baby.

All babies NEED lots of things to grow healthy and strong.

Put a tick against the things that all babies NEED:

- ☐ to be fed
- ☐ to be held
- ☐ to be hugged
- ☐ to be loved
- ☐ to be safe
- ☐ to be talked to
- ☐ to be rocked
- ☐ to be sung to
- ☐ to cry
- ☐ to sleep
- ☐ to play
- ☐ to laugh
- ☐ to pee and poo
- ☐ to be bathed
- ☐ to be touched
- ☐ to learn new things
- ☐ to be soothed and comforted

I was a GOOD Baby!!

THIS IS MY FAMILY

Meet my family

Draw your family:

LOVE makes a FAMILY.

FAMILY VALUES

Children grow best in loving families. Every family is different. Families have values and rules that can be spoken or unspoken. It helps when you understand the values and rules in your family. Ask your parent to help you understand the values and rules in your family.

Who is in my family:

....

....

....

....

Our family's values:

....

....

....

....

Our family's rules:

....

....

....

....

Consequences for mistakes:

....

....

....

....

What rules are hard for you to follow?

....

....

....

....

If you could change something in your family, what would you change?

....

....

....

....

I learn values like kindness, respect and forgiveness in my family.

ALL MY FAVORITE THINGS

Fill in each box with all your favorite things in each category.

There is only one ME!! And here are all my favorite things!!

There is only one me in the world!

We're the same and different

The MOST important ingredient in every family is LOVE. All families have angry, hurt and sad feelings sometimes. What is most important is that family members care about each other and love each other. Some children don't look like their parents and some children have parents who are older. List all the things that are the SAME about you and your family and then list all the things that are DIFFERENT about you and your family.

Ways we're the same:

Ways we're different:

Sometimes not looking like your parents or family is hard.
You are the same and different!!

ME AND MY SENSES

YOUR body and mind experiences and understands the world through your five senses. What you see. What you smell. What you taste. What you touch or feel. What you hear. Complete each box to learn about your 5 senses.

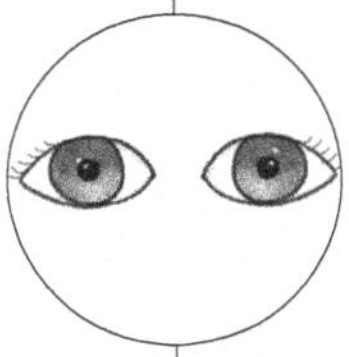

Sense of sight

These are five things my eyes can see:

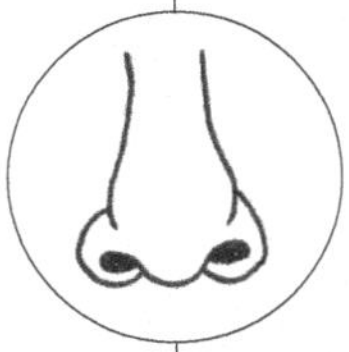

Sense of smell

These are five things I can see:

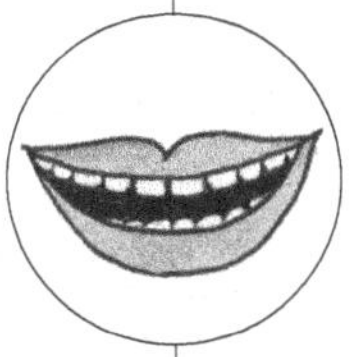

Sense of taste

These are five things I can taste:

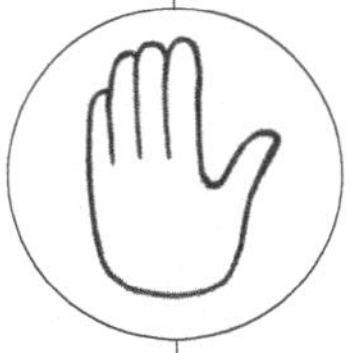

Sense of touch

These are five things I can touch:

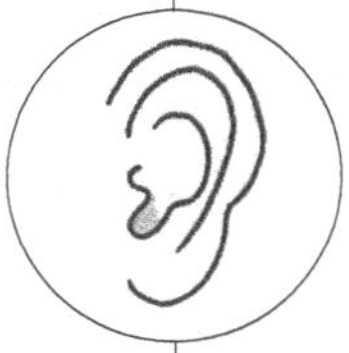

Sense of sound

These are five things I can hear:

5—4—3—2—1

YOUR body is amazing! Your five senses are working all the time to help you understand yourself and the world. Sometimes you might feel upset, hurt or angry because you didn't get to do something you really wanted to do. Or maybe someone said something that hurt your feelings. Your body and mind can begin to feel upset, scared, hurt or angry. Here's an activity that you can use to learn how to feel calm and safe inside your body. Practice this activity to help all the senses in your body feel safe, secure and relaxed. Next time you're upset, practice calming your five senses by using 5—4—3—2—1.

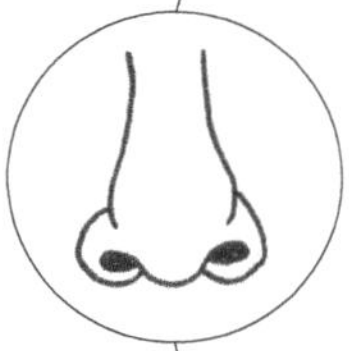

5—Take five deep breaths

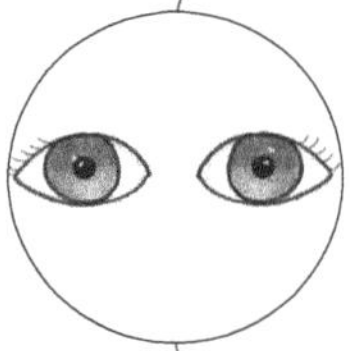

4—Name four things you can see

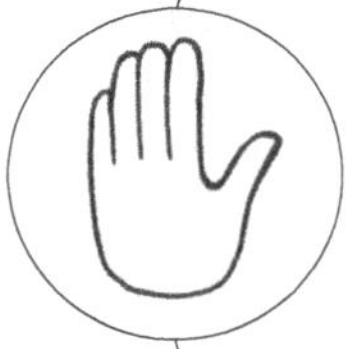

3—Name three things you can touch

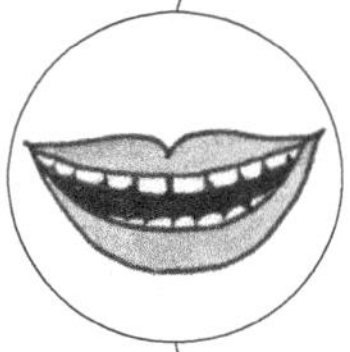

2—Name two things you love to taste

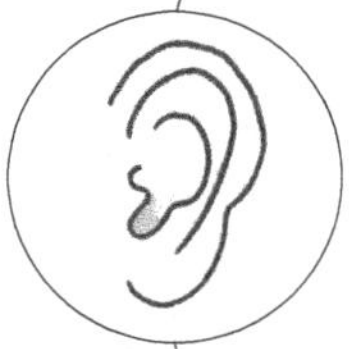

1—Name one thing you can hear

It feels good to relax and calm my busy body and mind!

MY HAPPY GARDEN

Did you know you have a Happy Garden? Think of all the things that make you feel happy and put a BIG smile on your face. In the flower garden below, write down all the things that make YOU happy. Color the flowers and imagine yourself watering those flowers to help your Happy Garden grow stronger and happier each day.

Every day I like spending time in my Happy Garden!

MY GIVING HEART

Did you know your heart likes to give love in lots of different ways? You do lots of things every day to show people that you care about them. The more love you give to others, the more people know that you care about them. Color all the things in your Giving Heart that you do to give your love to people you care about.

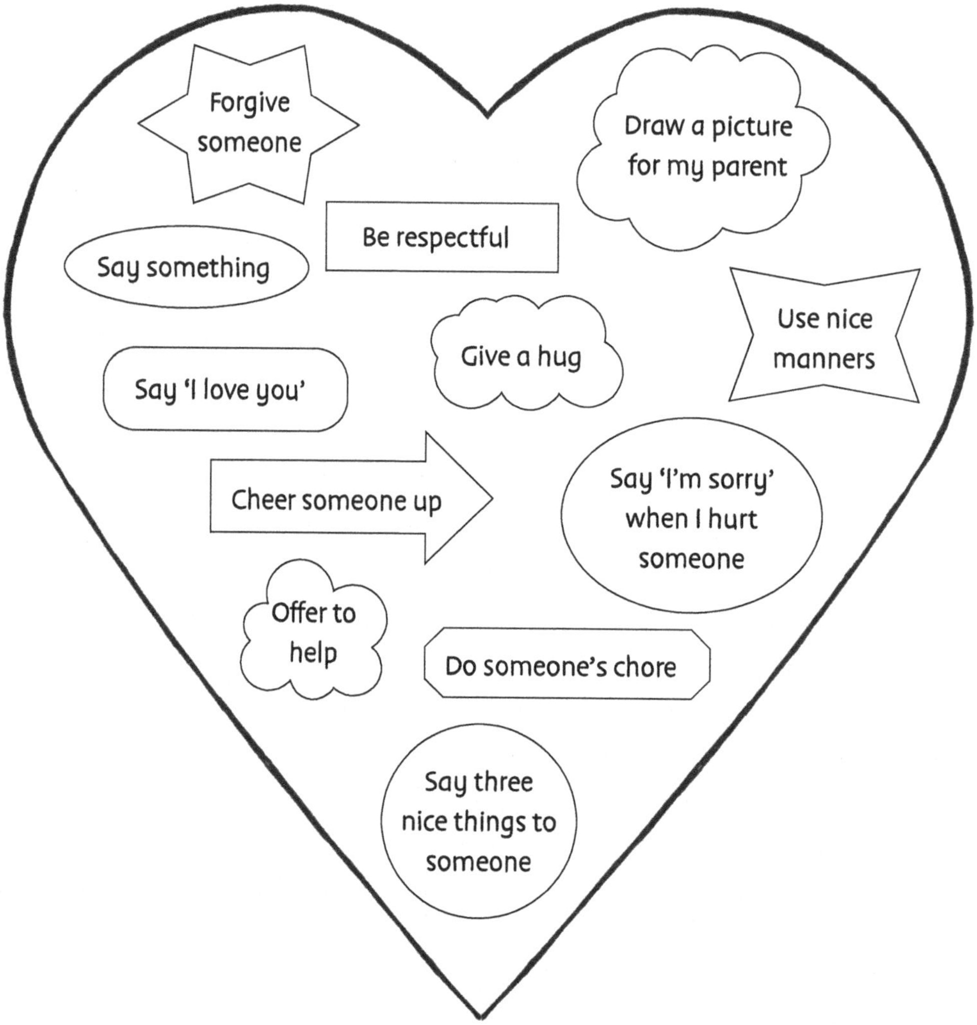

I do these things to give my love to the people I care about:

....

....

....

my heart has lots of love to give to all the people I care about!

MY RECEIVING HEART

Did you know your heart likes to give and receive love? Sometimes if you're adopted or in foster care and you've been through some difficult and painful experiences, it can be hard to keep your heart open to receiving love from other people. Your heart needs to feel cared about and loved. It's important to let love into your heart. Color all the things in your Receiving Heart.

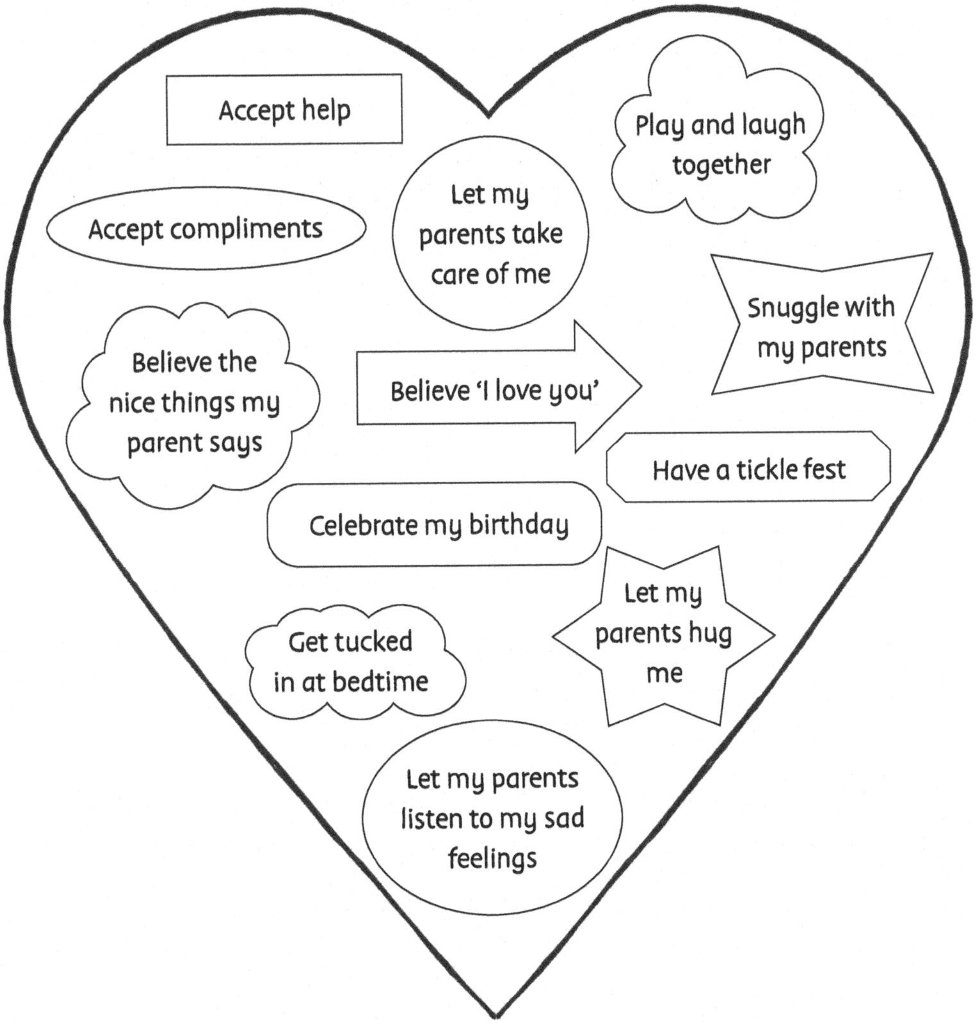

These are some more things my Receiving Heart needs to feel loved:

....

....

....

my heart deserves to be filled with lots of LOVE!

CHILDREN

THE STAGES OF ME!

YOU were born like everybody else. ALL babies start the same way. It takes a man and a woman to make a baby. The baby grows inside the woman's womb. Sometimes the man and woman who made the baby are not able to give their baby everything the baby needs to feel safe and grow strong and healthy. For some reason your birth parents or first parents couldn't take good care of a baby or child. All babies and children need someone who can parent them every day and do all the things that all babies and children need to grow and thrive. Parents who can feed them, cuddle with them, change their dirty diaper, play with them, teach them, protect them, hold them and help them grow big and strong.

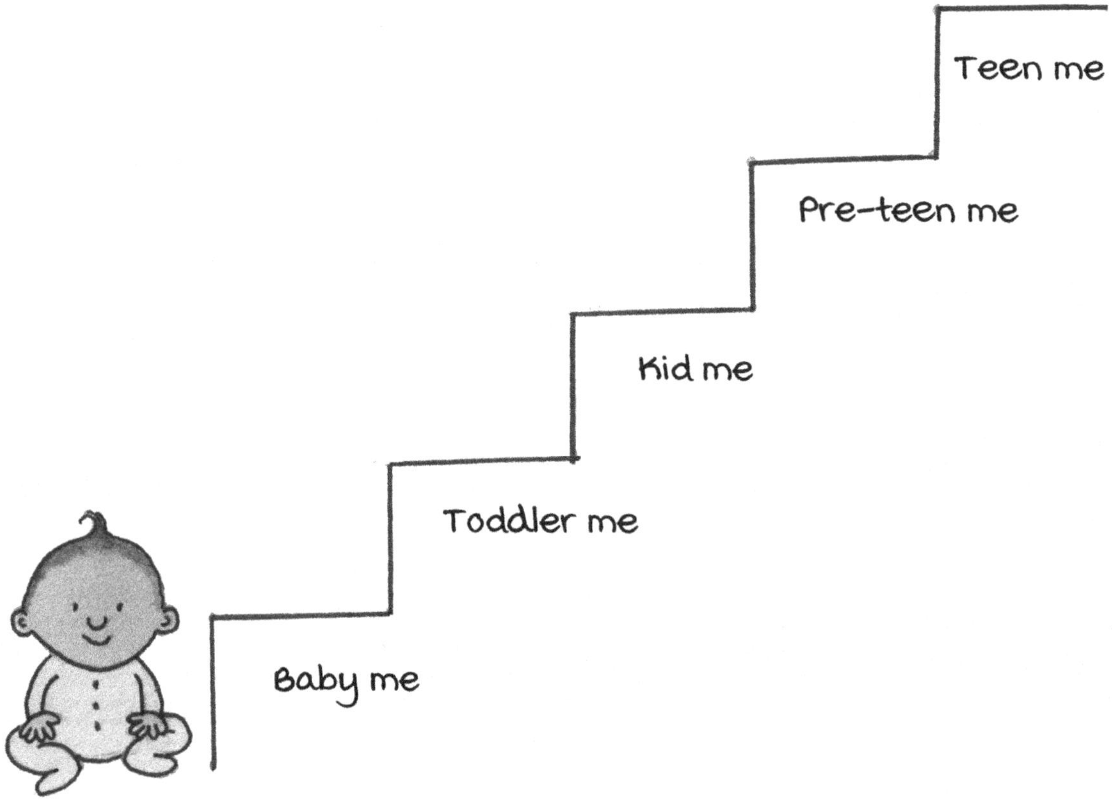

Each time you have a birthday, YOU get older, stronger and smarter!

Check all the things you did when you were a baby:

- ☐ Drank from a bottle
- ☐ Babbled and cooed
- ☐ Ate with my hands
- ☐ Pooped in a diaper
- ☐ Crawled a lot
- ☐ Ate in a highchair
- ☐ Slept in a crib
- ☐ Cried when I was hungry
- ☐ Sucked my thumb or a pacifier
- ☐ Cried a lot
- ☐ Drooled
- ☐ Played peek-a-boo

Now that you are BIGGER, you have learned to do LOTS more things:

- ☐ Talk and sing
- ☐ Brush my teeth
- ☐ Help with chores
- ☐ Run and jump
- ☐ Give good hugs
- ☐ Get myself dressed
- ☐ Ride a bike
- ☐ Read a book
- ☐ Color a picture
- ☐ Play games
- ☐ Potty in the toilet
- ☐ Build a fort
- ☐ Make my bed
- ☐ Make a friend
- ☐ Give a compliment

Soon in the future, you might even be able to do these things:

- ☐ Write a poem
- ☐ Play chess
- ☐ Join a club
- ☐ Play sports
- ☐ Have a sleepover
- ☐ Volunteer
- ☐ Do hard math problems
- ☐ Go to camp
- ☐ Talk about my feelings
- ☐ Skateboard
- ☐ Learn guitar
- ☐ Cook a meal
- ☐ Swim
- ☐ Get a phone
- ☐ Care for animals
- ☐ Apologize when I'm wrong
- ☐ Solve a conflict
- ☐ Go on a rollercoaster

I'm learning new things and growing stronger every day.

TOO MANY QUESTIONS?

When you're adopted or in foster care you get asked a LOT of questions!

How are you supposed to know all the answers to these tricky questions?

And these questions may remind you of how hard it feels sometimes to be adopted or in foster care.

How do you feel when you get asked questions about adoption or foster care? Tick all those that apply to how you feel.

☐ Happy	☐ Sad	☐ Proud	☐ Nervous
☐ Scared	☐ Anxious	☐ Excited	☐ Surprised
☐ Confident	☐ Playful	☐ Irritated	☐ Relaxed
☐ Upset	☐ Helpless	☐ Confused	☐ Worried

It's hard to answer questions when you're feeling confused, surprised, sad or worried.

Always remember:

- YOUR story, and all the parts of your story, belong to YOU.
- You get to decide what parts of your story you want to share.
- It's OK to not share the details of your story.
- It's OK to share your story with people you trust and love.
- It's OK to tell people that your story is personal and private.

my story belongs to me!

LET'S GET REAL!

When you're adopted or in foster care things can get confusing. Sometimes people use the term 'real mother' or 'real father' or 'real parents' when they're talking about your birth or first parents. Let's Get Real! You may have birth or first parents, foster parents, stepparents and/or adoptive parents – and they are all real! The birth or first mother who gave birth to you will always be your real birth or first mother. The mothers or fathers who are parenting you every day and helping you grow big and strong are also your real mothers and fathers.

Here is a drawing or picture of my real birth mother. Her name is ....

Here is a drawing or picture of my real birth father. His name is ....

Here is a drawing or picture of my real adoptive, foster or grandparents.
Their names are ....

It's OK to love ALL my REAL parents!

CHILDREN

WHY DID THIS HAPPEN?

There are many reasons why birth or first parents cannot take care of their child. Sometimes when a baby is born, parents are not ready or able to do all the things that a baby needs to grow healthy and strong. Sometimes parents have BIG grown-up problems and they may not even be able to take care of themselves. Grown-up problems like addiction to drugs or alcohol, homelessness, mental illness, violence and abuse, prison or crime, or being too young or not ready to be a parent. It's important to know and understand what were the BIG grown-up problems that your birth or first parents had that led to your needing a new family. Sometimes kids might blame themselves or think it's their fault that they were in foster care or adopted. Please talk to your parents and ask them all the questions you have about WHY your birth or first parents weren't able to be your everyday parents.

List some of the reasons why your birth or first parents were not able to take care of you as a baby or child:

1. ....

....

2. ....

....

3. ....

....

4. ....

....

5. ....

....

my story belongs to me! It's important for me to understand that what happened wasn't my fault!

ALL THE PLACES I'VE LIVED!

Here's a picture of my favorite place I've lived

Sometimes babies and children move too many times. Moving a lot is really hard on babies and children. With each move, kids lose things that are important to them. They lose family members, siblings, pets, friends, toys, routines, and sometimes they even lose a whole country, language and culture. It can feel really sad, scary and overwhelming to move so many times and to have so many changes in parents and caregivers.

Check all the different places you have lived and the people you have lived with:

☐ My first parents	☐ A group home	☐ A neighbor's home	☐ A car
☐ Foster parents	☐ An aunt or uncle	☐ A treatment center	☐ Other
☐ Grandparents	☐ Adoptive parents	☐ A shelter	
☐ An orphanage	☐ A hospital	☐ Another foster home	

I am an important part of my family!!

MY MISSING CLOUD

It's OK to think about people you care about and miss. If you lived with your birth or first parents and your brothers and sisters, you may think about them and miss them. If you lived with foster parents, or your grandparents, or an aunt or uncle, you may miss them too. You may have a teacher, a coach, a neighbor or a pet that you think about and miss. Write down the people you miss inside YOUR Missing Cloud!

Things you can do!

Start a Life Book with keepsakes, pictures and memories	Share your memories and feelings with someone you love	Create a memory box and draw or write your memories
Start a journal or a diary about your thoughts and feelings	Remember the people you miss in your prayers	Write a song or poem about the people you miss

It's OK to miss people I love and care about!

LET'S TALK!

Sometimes we just need to talk! It's good to have choices about what kinds of things you want to talk about. Circle all the things you want to talk about and find someone who cares about your thoughts and feelings so that YOU can share what's in your heart and mind!

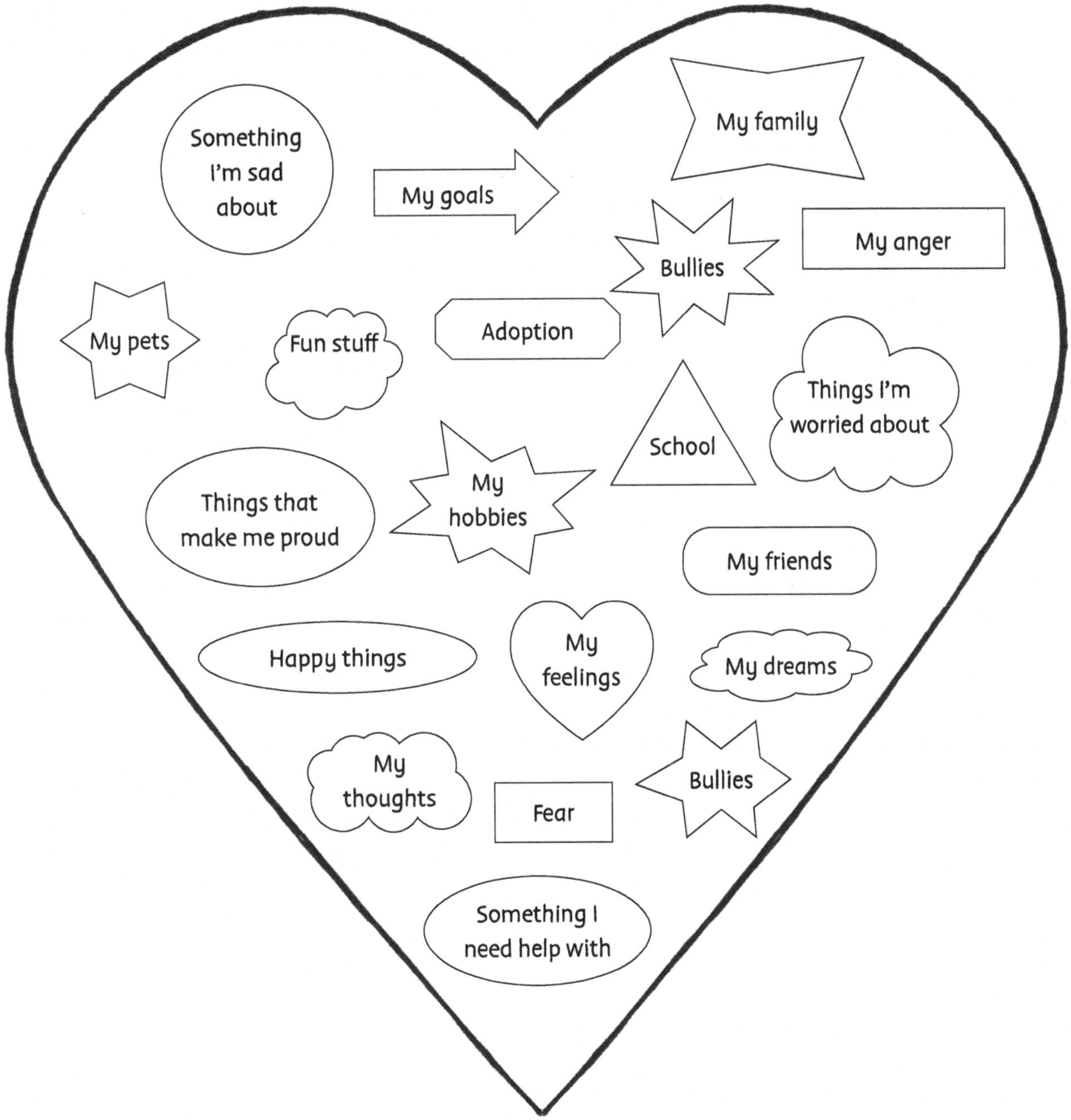

Sharing what's inside my heart and mind with people I trust and care about helps me feel loved and connected!

MY BIG WORRIES

Sometimes kids who are adopted or in foster care have BIG worries!

Have you ever had BIG worries like the ones these kids have?

Write down your BIG worries.

I worry that ....

I worry that ....

I worry that ....

Sometimes kids who are adopted or in foster care think those things because their birth or first parents couldn't take good care of them and keep them safe. But NONE of those things are true.

Here's what is true:

- YOU are good!
- YOU are loveable!
- NONE of the bad things that happened to you are your fault!
- YOU are likeable!
- We are so happy that you were born!

Find a grown-up who can tell you how much YOU are loved and cared about!

ALL MY HEART STRINGS

Did you know that your heart has heart strings? Your heart is connected to all the people who love you and all the people you love. As you grow bigger, your heart grows bigger and you love more people. You can love people you don't see any more and even people who have died. You can love more than one mom and more than one dad.

Write down all of your heart strings.

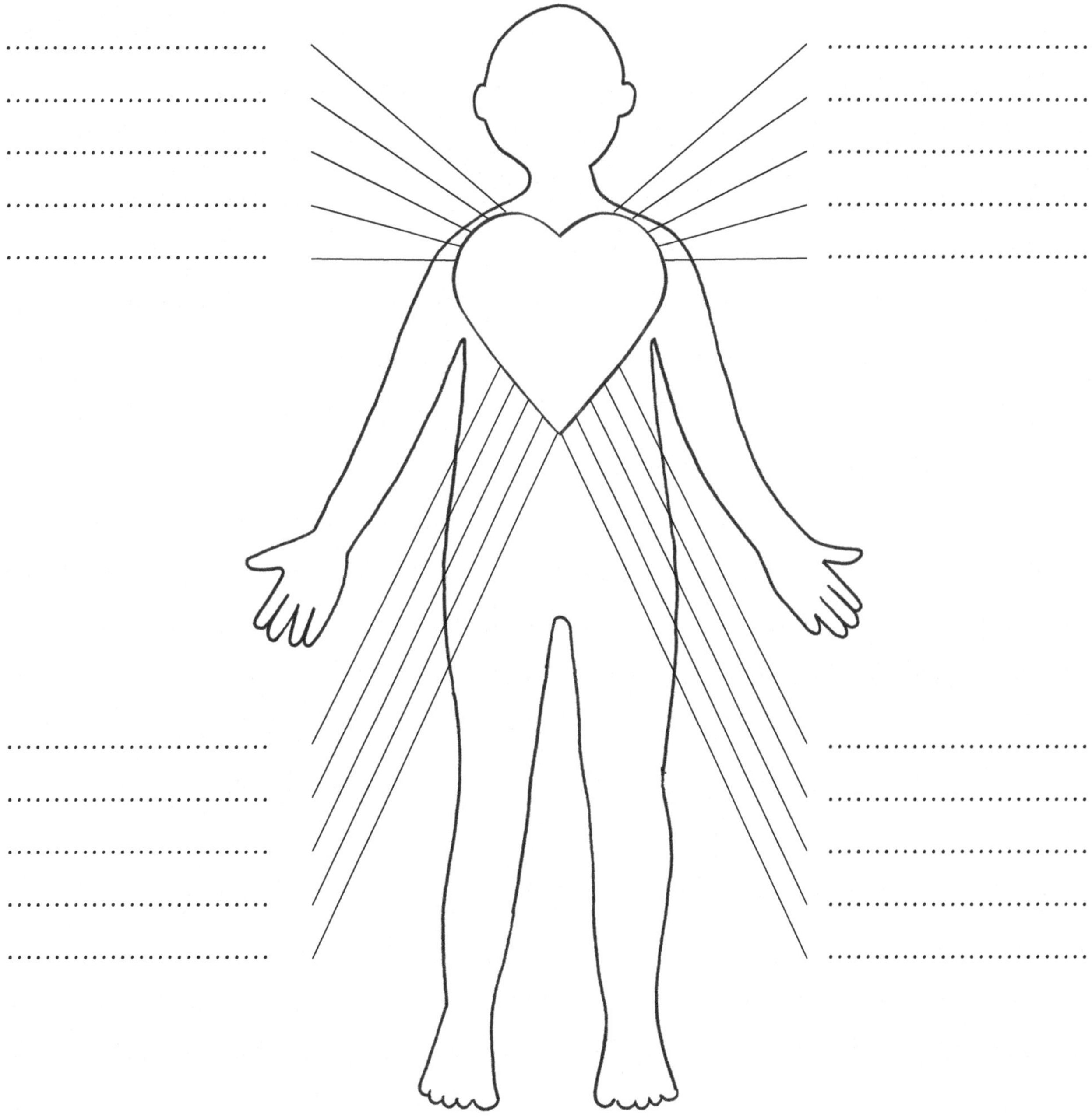

my heart is big and strong and deserves to be loved!

ONE AMAZING ME!

Most children are raised by the parents who created them. Children who are adopted are created and genetically connected to their birth or first mother and father. When they're adopted, they gain new parents who take on the role of being their mommy and/or daddy.

You are a blend of all the parents who helped to make you. You get certain things from your birth or first parents, like your beautiful eyes, skin and hair. Some of your personality traits come from the genes you inherited from your birth or first parents, for example if you're active or shy, or athletic or creative.

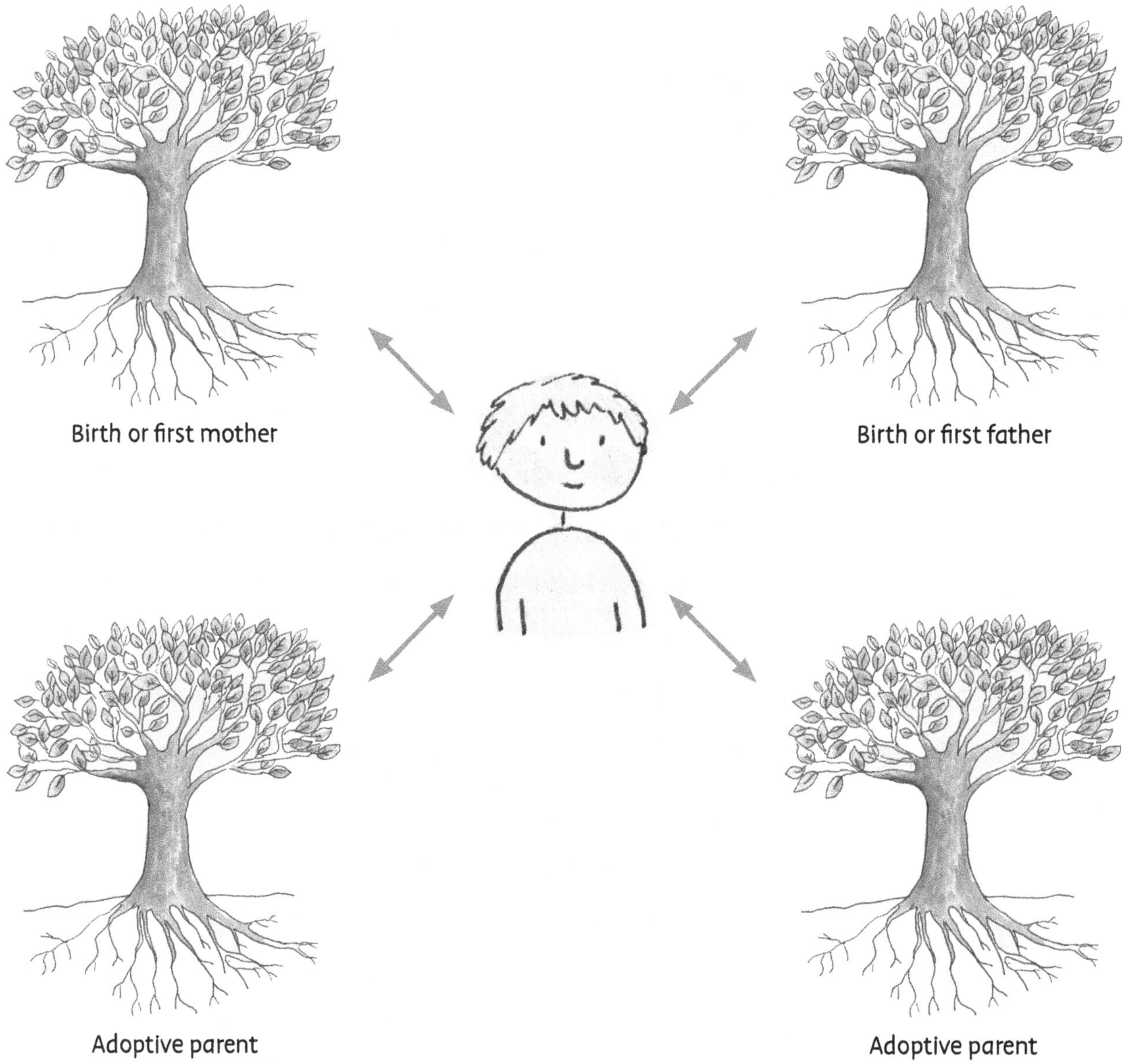

YOU are UNIQUE! There is only one YOU on this planet!

In the boxes below, draw pictures of all the parents who helped to make

One Amazing me!

My birth or first mother

My birth or first father

My adoptive parent

My adoptive parent

CHILDREN

THE LANGUAGE OF EMOTION

All humans have lots and lots of feelings. Our bodies and hearts are made to feel lots of different kinds of emotions. Some feelings are easier to feel, like happiness, love and excitement. Other feelings can be harder to feel, like fear, hurt and anger. What's most important for you to know is that ALL your feelings are OK to feel and express. Most kids need help learning all the right ways to express their feelings, especially the BIG feelings that can be overwhelming and scary sometimes. Circle ALL the feelings you have felt at different times of your life.

HAPPY

- Excited
- Cheerful
- Energetic
- Playful
- Silly
- Loving
- Creative

SAD

- Upset
- Tearful
- Bored
- Tired
- Guilty
- Depressed
- Hopeless

STRONG

- Secure
- Confident
- Empowered
- Curious
- Unique
- Brave

CALM

- Peaceful
- Relaxed
- Trusting
- Hopeful
- Valuable
- Safe
- Thoughtful

ANGRY

- Frustrated
- Annoyed
- Irritated
- Mad
- Furious
- Enraged

HURT

- Rejected
- Abandoned
- Punished
- Abused
- Lonely
- Ashamed

ANXIOUS

- Worried
- Nervous
- Stressed
- Confused
- Inadequate
- Embarrassed

SCARED

- Fearful
- Alone
- Overwhelmed
- Hurt
- Helpless
- Lost
- Invisible

Learning how to express BIG feelings takes practice!

WHAT'S IN MY HEART

YOUR heart is filled with all the different feelings you've felt your whole life. Fill your heart with all the different kinds of feelings you have experienced. Use different color crayons or colored pencils to represent the different kinds of feelings that are in YOUR HEART.

Check any of the boxes below if you feel these emotions.

☐ Happy	☐ Proud	☐ Excited	☐ Lonely	☐ ....
☐ Loved	☐ Calm	☐ Hurt	☐ Confused	☐ ....
☐ Angry	☐ Sad	☐ Scared	☐	☐ ....

my heart is BIG and STRONG!

MY FEELINGS BODY

We all have feelings inside our body. All our feelings are OK. Where do you feel all the different feelings? Write or colour all the different feelings in your body. In the lists below, put a check against any feelings that you have.

- ☐ Happy
- ☐ Loved
- ☐ Proud
- ☐ excited

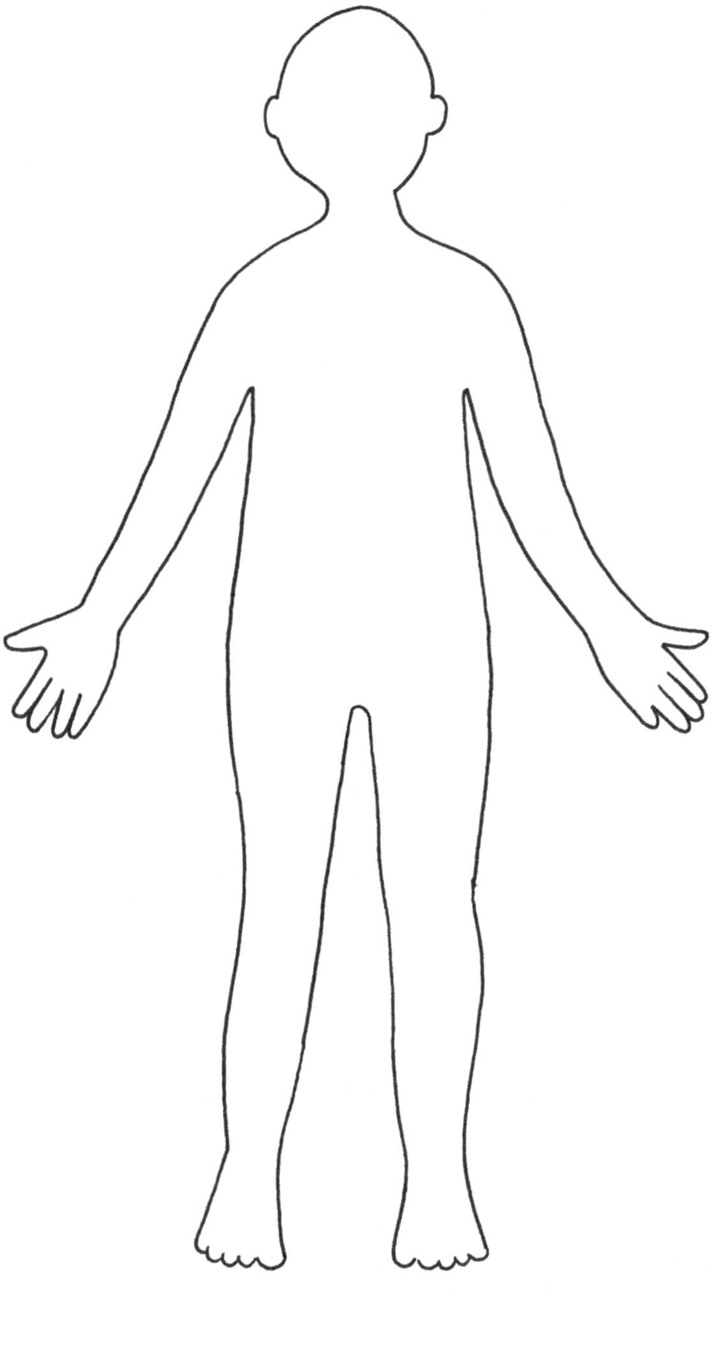

- ☐ Sad
- ☐ Hurt
- ☐ Afraid
- ☐ Stressed

- ☐ Silly
- ☐ Calm
- ☐ Curious
- ☐ Brave
- ☐ Safe
- ☐ Hopeful

- ☐ Worried
- ☐ Lonely
- ☐ Angry
- ☐ Rejected
- ☐ Confused
- ☐ Overwhelmed

my body belongs to me. my body is growing and learning every day!

SOMETIMES I FEEL HAPPY

A picture of my happy feelings

Things that make me feel happy:

I feel happy when ....

I feel happy when ....

I feel happy when ....

I feel happy when ....

I feel happy when ....

I love to share my HAPPY feelings!

SOMETIMES I FEEL SAD

A picture of my sad feelings

Things that make me feel sad:

I feel sad when ....

I feel sad when ....

I feel sad when ....

I feel sad when ....

I feel sad when ....

It helps to get the SAD feelings out of my mind and body!

SOMETIMES I FEEL STRONG

A picture of my strong feelings

Things that make me feel strong:

I feel strong when ....

I feel strong when..

I feel strong when ....

I feel strong when ....

I feel strong when..

I like feeling STRONG in my body and mind! I make good choices for myself when I feel good about me!

SOMETIMES I FEEL LOVED

A picture of my loving feelings

Things that make me feel loved:

I feel loved when ....

I feel loved when..

I feel loved when ....

I feel loved when ....

I feel loved when ....

Feeling LOVED by people who care about me helps me know I'm special, valuable and important!

SOMETIMES I FEEL HURT

A picture of my hurt feelings

Things that make me feel hurt:

I feel hurt when..

I feel hurt when..

I feel hurt when..

I feel hurt when..

I feel hurt when..

It helps when I share my HURT feelings with people I love and trust!

SOMETIMES I FEEL CALM

A picture of my calm feelings

Things that make me feel calm:

I feel calm when ....

I feel calm when ....

I feel calm when ....

I feel calm when ....

I feel calm when ....

Getting rid of all the stress in my body and mind helps me to feel CALM and relaxed on the inside!

SOMETIMES I FEEL SCARED

A picture of my scared feelings

Things that make me feel scared:

I feel scared when ....

I feel scared when ....

I feel scared when ....

I feel scared when ....

I feel scared when ....

I feel better when I share my SCARED feelings with someone I trust and love!

SOMETIMES I FEEL MAD

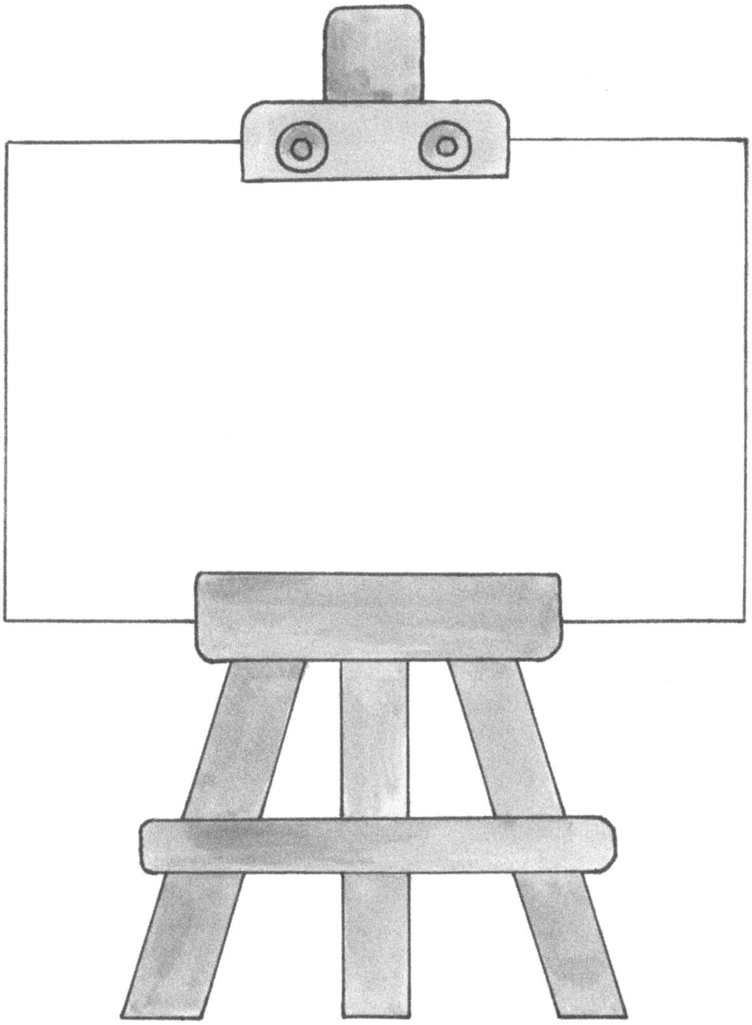

A picture of my mad feelings

Things that make me feel mad:

I feel mad when ....

I feel mad when ....

I feel mad when ....

I feel mad when ....

I feel mad when ....

HURT feelings and MAD feelings go together!

MY FEELINGS PIE

Being adopted or in foster care can create lots of different kinds of feelings. Making your Feelings Pie can help you understand all the different feelings YOU have about being adopted or in foster care. Which feelings get a big, medium or small slice of pie? Use different colors to represent all the different feelings in your Feelings Pie! Share your Feelings Pie with someone you love and trust!

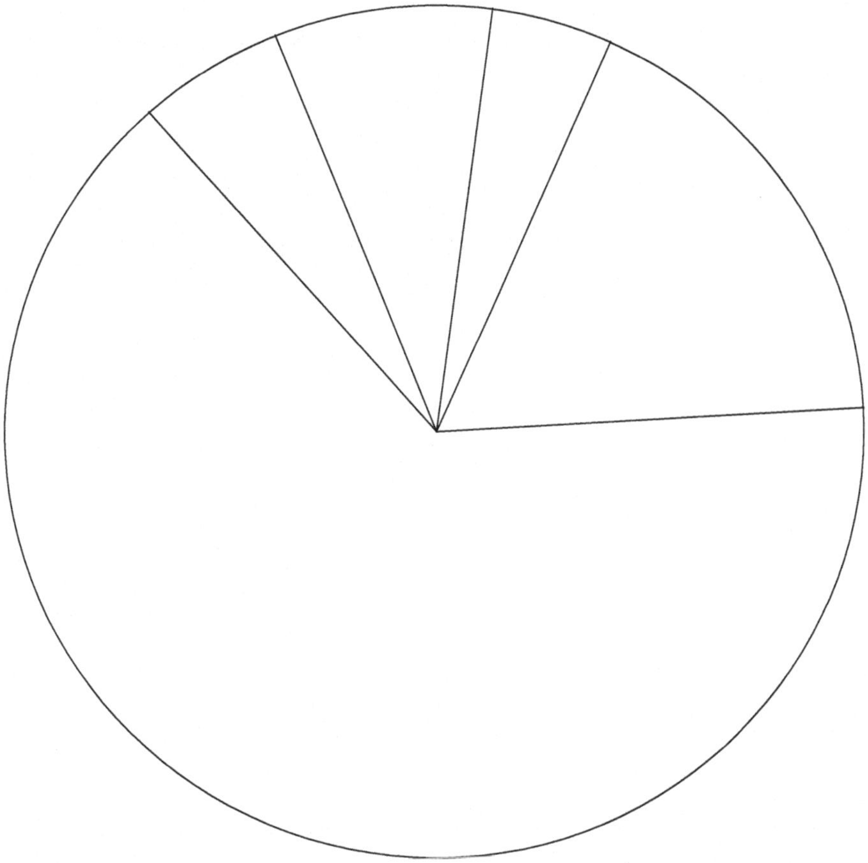

Put a check against all the emotions you have felt and add any others that you might feel.

☐ Happy	☐ Relaxed	☐ Scared	☐ Anxious	☐ Loved
☐ Sad	☐ Confused	☐ Playful	☐ Worried	☐ Lonely
☐ Hurt	☐ Angry	☐ Proud	☐ Excited	☐ Thankful
☐	☐	☐	☐	☐ ....

Expressing ALL my feelings is important!

MY WORRY BUBBLE

Everybody worries sometimes! It helps if we get those worries out of our head and into the Worry Bubble! Being adopted or in foster care can create worries such as 'Does my family **really** love me or want me?' or 'Will I have to move again?' Or other worries like missing your first family, or missing your old foster family, or not living with your brother or sister, or wondering if your birth/first parents are OK. Now let's get YOUR worries out of your head and into the Worry Bubble!

I can share my Worry Bubble with someone I love and trust!

MY STRESS THERMOMETER

YOU experience STRESS in your body **and** your mind!

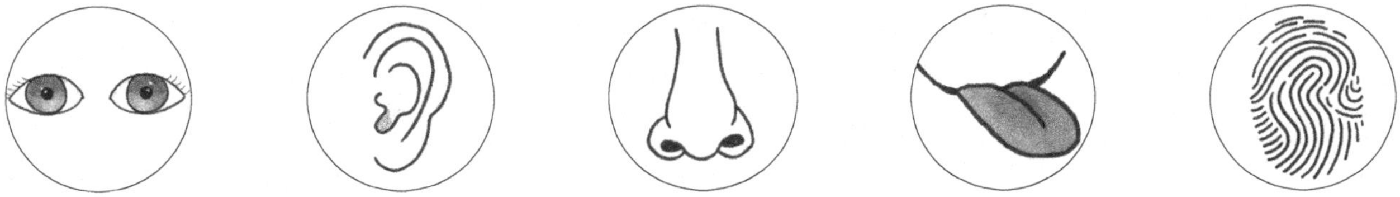

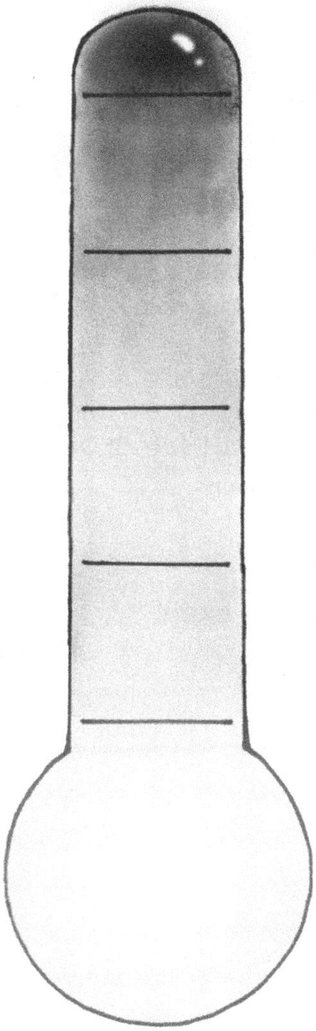

5. Feeling overwhelmed, toxic stress
'I'm overwhelmed and want to run, hide or get out of here'

4. Anger, agitation, frustration
'I'm feeling stressed, hurt, anxious or angry'

3. Feeling a bit irritated, I can feel my body and mind getting upset or stressed
'I'm feeling a little upset but I can handle it'

2. Having fun, feeling excited, playful, silly
'I'm happy and enjoying my day!'

1. Relaxed, focused, calm and peaceful
'My body and mind FEEL relaxed and calm. I'm good at listening and learning when my body and mind are calm and relaxed'

STRESS can make me feel scared and overwhelmed!

My plan to de-stress

When I notice my body feels stressed or anxious I can do things to help my body and mind feel better!

Five nice things I can do to de-stress my body:

1. ....
2. ....
3. ....
4. ....
5. ....

Five nice things I can do to de-stress my mind or thoughts:

1. ....
2. ....
3. ....
4. ....
5. ....

Use your Stress Thermometer to notice when your body and mind begin to get stressed. Use your De-Stress Plan to help your body and mind relax and calm down after something stressful happens.

It's easy to make good choices when my body is calm and relaxed!

MY ANGRY VOLCANO

We all get angry sometimes! We can get a little angry or a LOT angry! Learning to express our anger the right way takes practice. First, it's important to understand that we usually get angry when our feelings have been hurt or we're upset about something. Sometimes we can hold hurt or angry feelings inside our body and mind for a long time. It's really important to understand your own angry or hurt feelings so you can learn to express those feelings. In the Lava Pool below, list ALL the things that have happened in YOUR life that have hurt your feelings and made you feel hurt and angry.

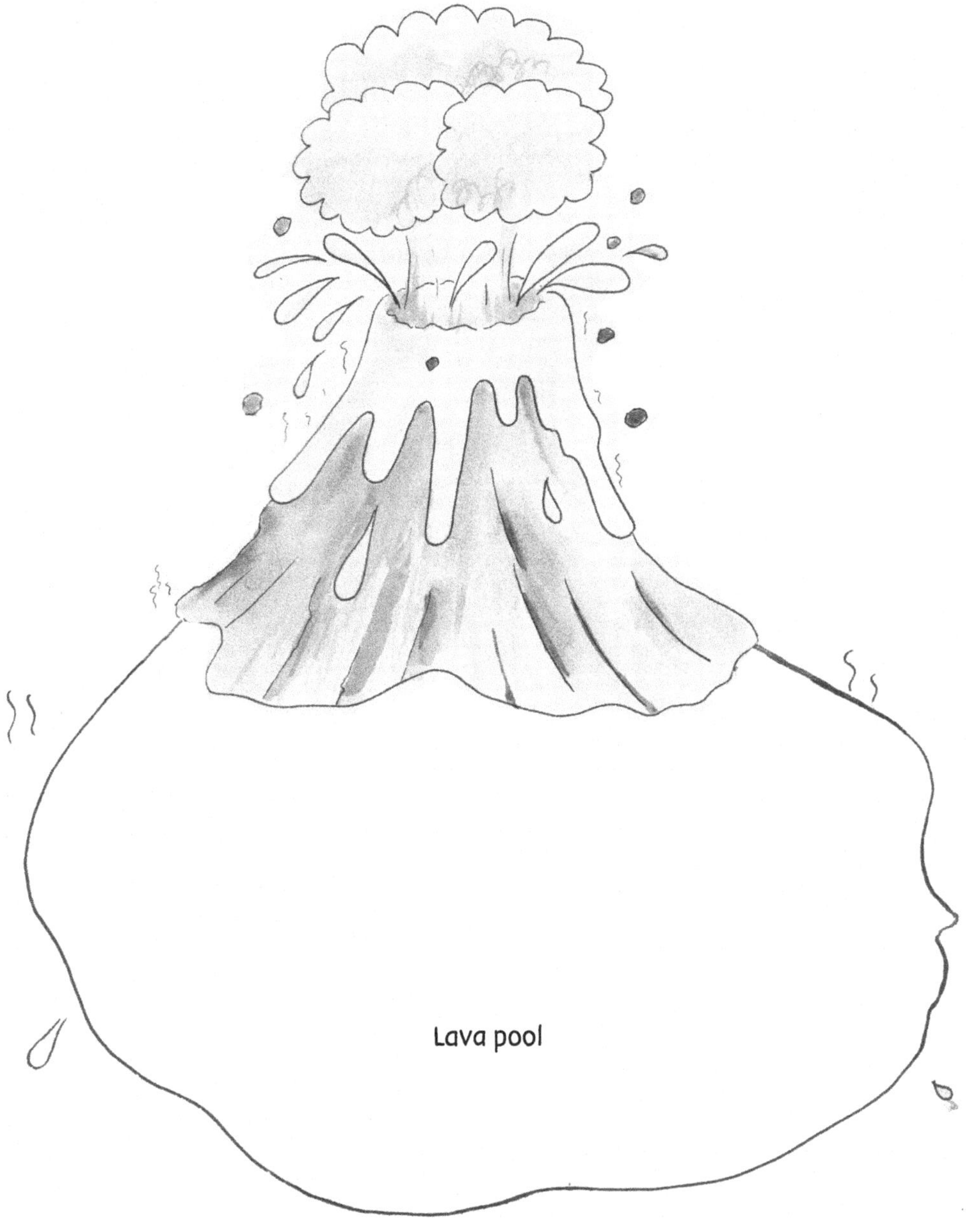

Learning to express ANGRY feelings takes practice!!

I WONDER!

Being adopted or in foster care means you have lots and lots of questions. You have a very smart brain that is supposed to have lots of questions about everything, including your foster care or adoption story.

Here are some of the questions that most kids have:

- Why was I in foster care and/or adopted?
- Why weren't my birth or first parents able to take care of me?
- What do my birth or first parents look like?
- Where are my birth or first parents now?
- Do I have brothers or sisters?
- Do my birth or first parents think about me or love me?
- Why did my parents want to adopt me?

What are some of the questions that you have about your birth or first family?

1. ....
2. ....
3. ....
4. ....
5. ....
6. ....
7. ....
8. ....
9. ....
10. ....
11. ....
12. ....
13. ....
14. ....
15. ....

Be Bold. Be Curious. Be YOU.

MY BIRTH OR FIRST MOTHER

My birth or first mother's name is .... She was born on .... Her birthplace is .... and her nationality is .... She has .... sisters and .... brothers. When I was born, she was .... years old.

Photo or drawing

Other things I know about her:

Things I wish I knew about her:

I don't live with her because ....

....

Sometimes when I think about her, I feel ....

....

It's OK to have questions and feelings about my birth or first mother!

MY BIRTH OR FIRST FATHER

My birth or first father's name is .... He was born on .... His birthplace is .... and his nationality is .... He has .... sisters and .... brothers. When I was born, he was .... years old.

Photo or drawing

Other things I know about him:

Things I wish I knew about him:

I don't live with him because ....

....

Sometimes when I think about him, I feel ....

....

It's OK to have questions and feelings about my birth or first father!

BROTHERS AND SISTERS IN MY BIRTH FAMILY

Many children who are adopted or are in foster care have also experienced being separated from their brothers or sisters. Being separated from your siblings is really hard. Brothers and sisters care about each other and miss each other when they can't grow up together. Use this page to stay in touch with your brothers and sisters.

	Name	Birthdate	Lives	Photo
1.	....	....	....	
2.	....	....	....	
3.	....	....	....	
4.	....	....	....	
5.	....	....	....	

Siblings matter! It's OK to miss and think about my brothers and sisters.

MY FAMILY AND FRIENDS

Family and friends are the people we choose to let into our hearts and that we care about even if we don't see them a lot. You may have an old foster parent, teacher, neighbor who felt like framily to you. Here are the names and pictures of my framily.

	Name	How I know them	Lives	Photo
1.	....	....	....	
2.	....	....	....	
3.	....	....	....	
4.	....	....	....	
5.	....	....	....	
6.	....	....	....	

Connections matter! I try and stay connected to people I care about!

THREE KINDS OF PROBLEMS

Did you know there are three kinds of problems? There are 'small' problems, like trying to decide what clothes to wear or when to do homework. There are 'medium-sized' problems, like getting into a fight or taking something that isn't yours. Then there are 'BIG' problems, like moving to a new family, having someone you love be addicted to drugs, or someone you care about who is really sick or dies. It's important to not feel alone with our problems. It's OK to ask a grown-up who loves and cares about you for help.

Here are some examples of small problems I have:

Here are some examples of medium-sized problems I have:

Here are some examples of BIG problems I have:

I feel overwhelmed when I'm alone with BIG problems.
It's OK to talk about my BIG problems and feelings!

REJECTION HURTS!

Feeling rejected by people we care about hurts. It's important to understand our own thoughts and feelings when something stressful happens and we feel rejected.

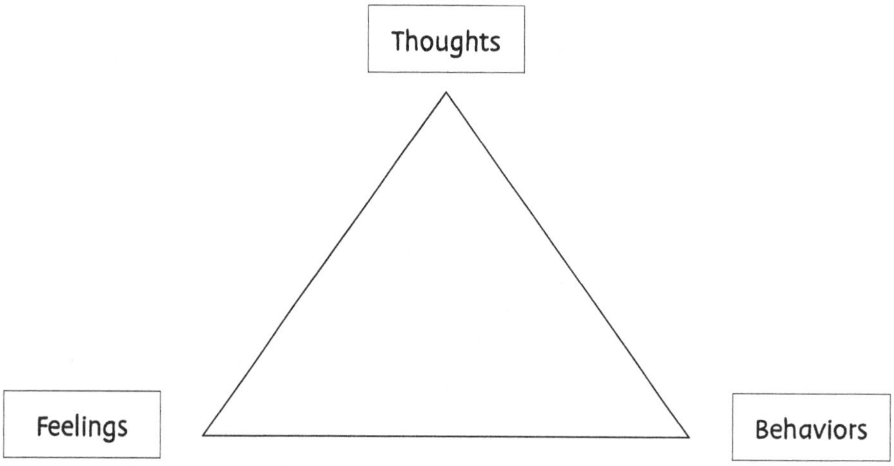

When something stressful happens at home and I feel rejected:

I think ....

....

I feel ....

....

I act this way ....

....

When something stressful happens at school and I feel rejected:

I think ....

....

I feel ....

....

I act this way ....

....

When something stressful happens with my friends and I feel rejected:

I think ....

....

I feel ....

....

I act this way ....

....

my thoughts, feelings and actions belong to me! When I understand my thoughts and feelings I can learn better ways to express myself!

WHAT'S THERAPY?

Child therapists help children learn about and understand their worries and feelings so they can feel better about themselves. Children who have been adopted or are in foster care have had some scary and hurtful things happen in their life. It doesn't mean there is anything broken, bad or damaged about them. Therapy helps us learn, grow and heal! Circle the things in the heart below that are true for you.

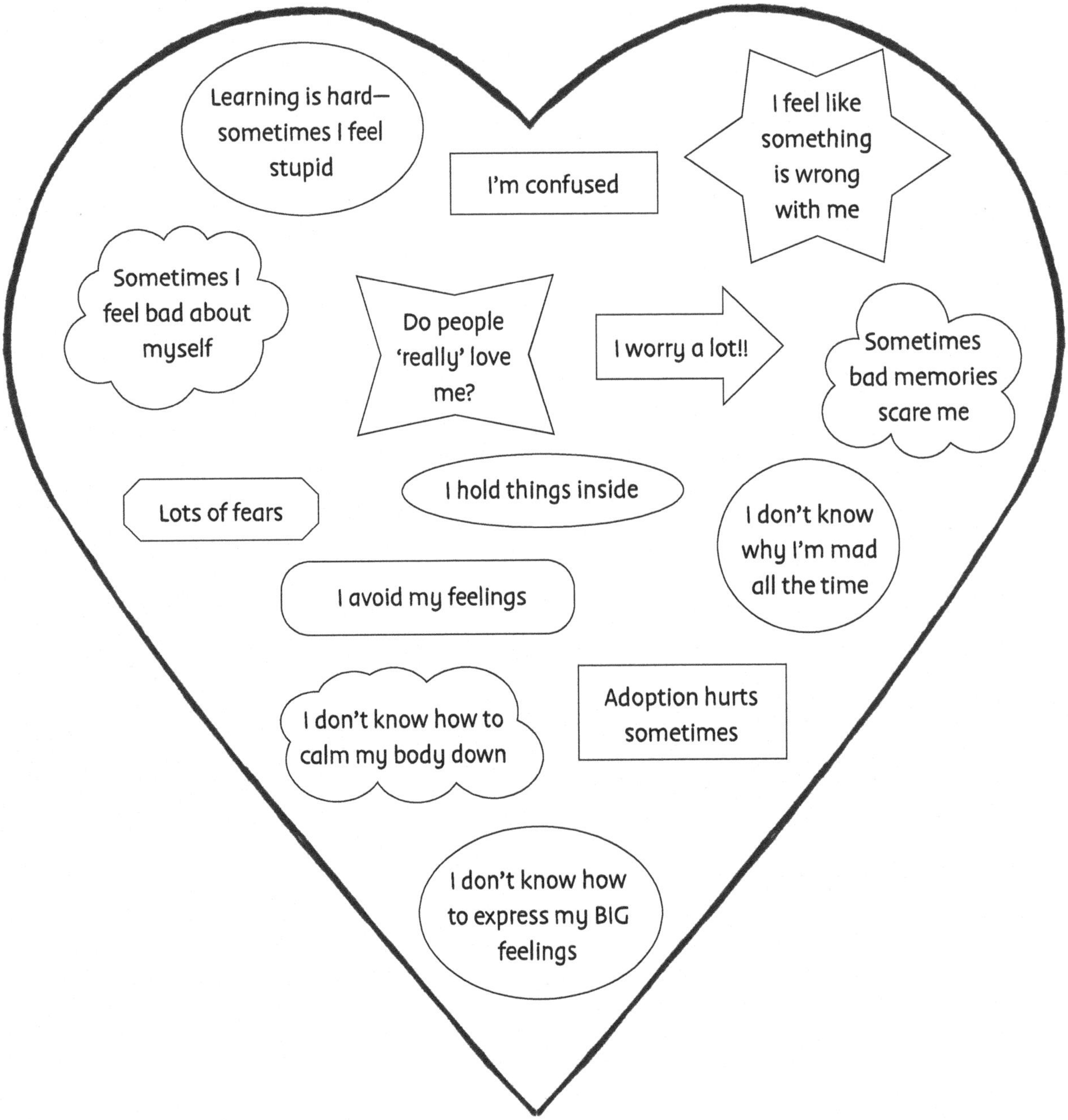

Learning how to understand and express feelings takes practice.

THIS IS MY FOSTER CARE STORY

First, it's **really important** to understand that it is NOT your fault that you are in foster care. When a home is not a safe place or parents are unable to take good care of a child, the baby or child may live in a foster family or an orphanage.

I was born on .... (date), in .... (city), ... (state), ... (country).

I weighed .... and I was born at .... (hospital).

My birth/first mother's name is ...., and she was .... years old when I was born. My birth/first father's name is ...., and he was .... years old when I was born.

When I was a baby, I lived with ....

I was placed in foster care when I was .... years old, because my parents had BIG grown-up problems like .... and .... and ....

When I was younger, I lived in .... different homes, shelters or orphanages, which was scary and confusing sometimes.

These are some of the good memories I have from foster care:

....

....

....

These are some of the bad memories I have from foster care:

....

....

....

When I was in foster care, the judge and social workers made decisions about what was best for me, like where I should live and who I should live with. Some children leave foster care and go back to live with their mom/dad/parents, other children live with their grandparents or other relatives, and some are adopted. This is what happened to me:

....

....

....

It's important to know and understand my foster care story!

THIS IS MY ADOPTION STORY

I was born on .... (date), in .... city), ... (state), ... (country).

I weighed .... and I was born at. .... (hospital).

My birth/first mother's name is ...., and she was .... years old when I was born. My birth/first father's name is ...., and he was .... years old when I was born.

I was .... years old when my family adopted me. Adoption can be confusing sometimes because I have a birth or first mother and a birth or first father, who made me but are not parenting me. And now I have my parents who adopted me. I have been told I was adopted because my birth or first parents were unable or unwilling to parent a child because ....

Sometimes I think I was adopted because:

....

....

Sometimes I don't like being adopted because:

....

....

My parents adopted me because:

....

....

It's important for me to understand my adoption story.

— PART 2 —

TEENS

CONTENTS

Hi Teen!

This book is all about YOU! YOUR life, YOUR beliefs, YOUR feelings, YOUR past, YOUR future and everything that has happened to YOU! The good stuff and the hard stuff!

EVERY part of your history and journey belongs to YOU.

As a teen, you're probably thinking a lot about your future, your past, and all the things that have happened in your life. Teens who are adopted or are in kinship or foster care think a lot about 'what happened' and 'why it happened' and may be searching for answers to all their questions and the missing parts of their history.

You should have a lot of questions, thoughts and feelings about all the things that have happened to you that changed and shaped your life. You've had more losses and challenges than the average teen.

One of the most important parts of being a teen is figuring out who you are and understanding all the different parts of your identity. For teens who are adopted or in foster care, this is no easy task! It requires a lot more focus, attention and emotional 'work' due to all the things you've been through.

YOU have a right to the truth of your story. The REAL story of what happened, why it happened and how it happened. Understanding the circumstances, events, decisions and the people connected to the earliest parts of your history will help you better understand yourself and help you create a strong identity and a positive future.

Remember to be kind and compassionate with yourself as you explore deeper issues and feelings. Finding YOUR authentic self is the key to a happy and meaningful life.

Be Bold. Be Curious. Be YOU!

— Chapter 1 —

LOSS

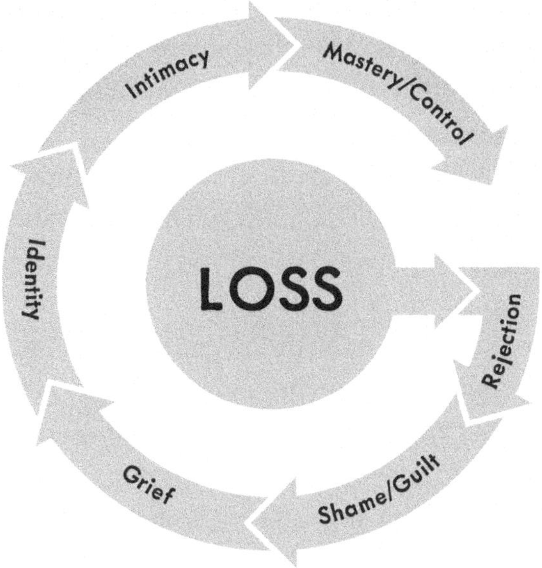

Loss and trauma begin the journey into adoption, foster or kinship care.

This workbook will help you learn about and explore the issues and feelings that are connected to adoption, foster or kinship care. The goal is to empower you to know and understand your story, your past, your identity and all the different parts of YOU. To help you explore the complex issues and feelings you may experience as you build your identity and who you are in this world. This is an activity workbook that will guide you through a process of self-exploration and self-reflection.

Loss begins the journey. It is a crisis or trauma that creates the circumstances that lead to a child's placement in foster care, kinship or adoption. It could be a crisis of an unplanned pregnancy, poverty, mental illness, addiction, divorce, rape, incest, or a country's crisis that results in war, refugees, natural disasters, epidemics and cultural biases and leads to the displacement of children. The Seven Core Issues are loss, rejection, shame/guilt, grief, identity, intimacy and mastery/control, and are created through the experience of foster care, kinship and adoption.

These issues are present any time a child is not being raised by the parents who created them, including infant adoptions, older child adoptions, kinship or guardianship families, foster families, step-families, third-party reproduction such as surrogacy and donor insemination, and both open and closed adoptions. The Seven Core Issues are 'normal' crisis issues, feelings and challenges that teens experience. The presence of these issues does NOT mean that you are abnormal, 'less than', broken or damaged. Rather, these are additional and expected emotions and challenges that come from the experience of being adopted or fostered.

Our culture has a long history of putting a 'positive spin' on adoption. Teens often hear how 'lucky' they are to have been 'chosen'. Parents often focus on the gains in adoption and may have difficulty exploring the losses or traumatic events connected to their teen's core issues. This can leave teens feeling confused as to why, even if they were adopted as a baby, they now feel hurt, overwhelmed, rejected and angry on the inside.

Teens may lose connections to both their maternal and paternal birth/first families, including siblings, grandparents, aunts, uncles and cousins. They may lose cultural, racial and ethnic connections and their language of origin and even their country of origin. If they are in foster care or adopted as an older child, they may also lose important friends, foster families, pets, schools, neighborhoods and familiar surroundings.

If you were adopted and lack genetic, medical, religious, cultural, ethnic, racial and other historical information about your birth/first family, you may want and need answers to questions that will help form your identity—things like where you come from, why your birth/first parents placed you or couldn't take care of you, and what became of those parents, or if you have siblings, and whether you look like or act like your birth/first parents, siblings or extended family.

Being a teen is one of the most exciting times in your life. It's the stage in life where you're focused on figuring out who you are, what you stand for, and what kind of life you want to live. For those of you who are adopted or in foster or kinship care, you have extra challenges because it's often harder to get some of the answers you may need to build your identity.

The ultimate goal for this workbook is to help YOU gain a sense of mastery, which is about regaining power and control over your life. Every human being needs to feel powerful. Feeling empowered helps you make positive and healthy decisions for yourself. When you feel disempowered, you may feel 'out of control' and you may have a strong need to 'fight for control'. This workbook will help you explore some of the underlying issues that may have left you feeling confused, isolated, overwhelmed, hurt or angry. Exploring and healing from these issues will help you see just how resilient and strong YOU really are! Achieving mastery takes work, yes emotional work. But believe me, YOU are worth it!

MY STRENGTHS JAR

Being adopted or in foster care means you've been through more challenges and losses than the average teen. It can be easy sometimes to get stuck with a lot of negative thoughts or feelings about yourself. It's really important to know that at every stage of your life, you were learning how to survive, how to cope, how to adapt, how to learn and how to be yourself. You have lots and lots of strengths. List ALL YOUR strengths in your Strengths Jar.

I am strong and resilient!

THE MYTHS IN ADOPTION, FOSTER CARE AND KINSHIP

There are a lot of myths and stereotypes about foster care and adoption. First, remember that YOU are the expert! Only you know what it feels like being adopted or in foster care because you have lived the experience. Some of the myths and stereotypes are listed below, with space for you to add some of your own:

- Children won't remember the bad things that happened to them.
- Children who are adopted or in kinship/foster care are 'lucky'.
- Children will forget about their birth/first parents.
- Attaching to new parents will be easy.
- Keeping children connected to their birth/first parents and prior attachments will confuse or upset them.
- Genetics don't matter.
- Children can only love one set of parents.
- Children don't remember, think about or yearn for the people they were attached to from their past.
- Racial, ethnic and cultural differences don't matter; we're color blind.
- If a child never met their siblings, those relationships don't really matter.
- Children will absorb and mirror the identity of their adoptive/foster/kinship parents.
- ?
- ?
- ?

I Am the writer of my own story!

ATTACHMENT AND RELATIONAL SELF-SURVEY

We all have strengths and challenges connected to how we were parented and cared for as a child. Learning to safely give and receive love and affection is no easy task when you've experienced early loss, trauma or attachment disruptions. There are no right or wrong answers. Identify your unique strengths and areas for growth.

Ranking: 1 being the lowest score and 5 being the highest.

1. I can understand the emotions, needs and concerns of other people, and pick up on their emotional cues.

   1 2 3 4 5

2. I feel comfortable socially and recognize the non-verbal, emotional cues in myself and others.

   1 2 3 4 5

3. As a teen, I know I want more independence and freedom. I'm able to maintain a healthy relationship with my parent/s as I'm working to become more responsible and independent.

   1 2 3 4 5

4. I am aware of my own non-verbal emotions and needs as these are key indicators of what I am really feeling and experiencing on the inside.

   1 2 3 4 5

5. When conflict arises, I can identify constructive ways to understand and resolve the conflict, which may include talking about difficult events and feelings.

   1 2 3 4 5

6. I believe that keeping connections to family, friends and other people and things I care about is meaningful and enhances a positive sense of identity and belonging.

   1 2 3 4 5

7. I recognize my own internal 'emotional states' and how they affect my thoughts, perceptions, behaviors and relationships.

   1 2 3 4 5

Each day is a new opportunity to learn something new about myself!

8. I know how to develop and maintain meaningful, authentic relationships. I know what my needs are and can communicate them clearly to people I trust.

1 2 3 4 5

9. After a stressful event or conflict, I can emotionally bounce back and find inner calm.

1 2 3 4 5

10. I am aware of my own attachment style/pattern as it impacts every aspect of my intimate relationships with family, friends, coaches, teachers, and so on.

1 2 3 4 5

11. As a teen, I know that I'll make mistakes as I'm figuring out who I am and what I want to do with my life. I can easily forgive myself when I make a mistake.

1 2 3 4 5

12. It's easy for me to get close to others. I am comfortable depending on others and having them depend on me. I don't worry about abandonment or becoming too close to others.

1 2 3 4 5

13. As a teen, I'm still learning how much of my story and my history I want to share with others. It's OK to keep parts of my story private and it's OK to share the parts of my story that I decide I'm comfortable sharing.

1 2 3 4 5

14. When I'm feeling distressed or overwhelmed, I have the emotional skills and supportive relationships to manage my intense feelings and return to calmness. My increased emotional intelligence helps me express my painful/hurt/sad/angry emotions and think through various coping strategies that are best for me.

1 2 3 4 5

15. I am able to accept my own imperfections and the imperfections of others. I can forgive myself, and others, when mistakes are made and I look for ways to solve problems that strengthen my connections to people I care about.

1 2 3 4 5

It's OK to make mistakes in relationships.
Learning to Love and Heal takes practice!

MY LOSSES JAR

Being adopted or in foster care always brings a lot of losses. There are losses that are experienced at the time when you were removed from your birth/first parents and there are losses that unfold as you grow, learn and develop. List all the losses you can think of connected to your adoption or foster care experiences.

my story belongs to me!

FOUR KINDS OF LOSSES IN ADOPTION, FOSTER AND KINSHIP CARE

Core losses

The original core losses in foster care, kinship and adoption are lifelong and intergenerational. The core traumatic experience of losing both your maternal and paternal family connections, race/culture/ethnic heritage and genetic or biological mirroring creates additional challenges in identity formation. They are experienced as traumatic events that strike at the center of a person's being. These core losses alter your life path and change how you feel about yourself and the world. The long-term ramifications cannot be fully understood at the time of the loss.

Secondary losses

These losses stem from the core losses and are experienced in your day-to-day lives. They show up on Mother's Day, or birthdays or when someone asks, 'Why are you adopted?' or, 'Why don't you look like your parents?' Secondary losses often surprise or trigger us as they show up in our everyday lives. These secondary losses surface and can intensify in adolescence when we may feel more deeply and abstractly about ourselves and the things that matter to us.

Ambiguous losses

These are losses that you experience that have no closure, no grief rituals or acknowledgement of what was lost. This can leave you stuck in grief or pain and searching for answers. These losses are difficult to grieve when they have not been identified, validated or emotionally supported. It is like having people disappear from your life. It can feel as if those people died, and yet there are no gravestones or rituals to help you grieve, mourn and recover from those losses.

Vicarious losses

These losses stem from traumatic memories and painful experiences, like moving from one family to another, or never seeing someone you loved and cared about. They can easily be retriggered during times of distress and cause sensory overload. These vicarious losses can live in sensory memory outside your conscious awareness and create feelings of confusion, anxiety and overwhelm.

UNDERSTANDING MY LOSSES

Use the Four Kinds of Losses in Adoption, Foster and Kinship Care to specifically identify YOUR losses. Understanding your losses is a really important part of understanding how being adopted or fostered has impacted you, how you feel about yourself and your own identity.

My core losses

My core losses are:

....
....
....
....
....
....
....

My secondary losses

My secondary losses are:

....
....
....
....
....
....
....

My ambiguous losses

My ambiguous losses are:

....
....
....
....
....
....
....

My vicarious losses

My vicarious losses are:

....
....
....
....
....
....
....

Understanding my losses is the first step towards healing!

MY LOSS HISTORY TIMELINE

Name: ....

Date: ....

Complete the Loss History Timeline by writing the year and placing an X by your age at the time of each loss you experienced. Losses may include people (family members, siblings, grandparents, foster parents, social workers, etc.), places and homes, pets, siblings, moves, and so on. For each X, write a brief description of the loss.

Year: ....

Age 0 3mos 6mos 9mos 1 2 3 4 5 6 7 8 9

Year: ....

Age 10 11 12 13 14 15 16 17 18 19

Brief description of my losses:

1. ....
2. ....
3. ....
4. ....
5. ....
6. ....
7. ....
8. ....
9. ....
10. ....
11. ....
12. ....

Use another sheet of paper if you have more losses.

MY LOSS HISTORY TIMELINE ACTIVITY

After completing your Loss History Timeline, review each loss and circle the ones that still hurt today. Think about those losses over time as you've grown and changed. Select a few of the losses that still cause hurt and pain today and complete the below activity.

Description of loss:	Describe how the loss impacts your life and relationships:
....	• .... • .... • .... • .... • ....
....	• .... • .... • .... • .... • ....
....	• .... • .... • .... • .... • ....
....	• .... • .... • .... • .... • ....

Big hurts can linger for a long time.

CORE LOSSES IMPACT THE MIND, HEART AND BODY

The traumatic losses you experienced connected to foster care and adoption affect your mind, heart and body. It is common to minimize or try and avoid the impact of the losses or traumatic events you have experienced. Acknowledging, understanding and healing from the impact of these losses takes a bit of work. Reflect on the questions below.

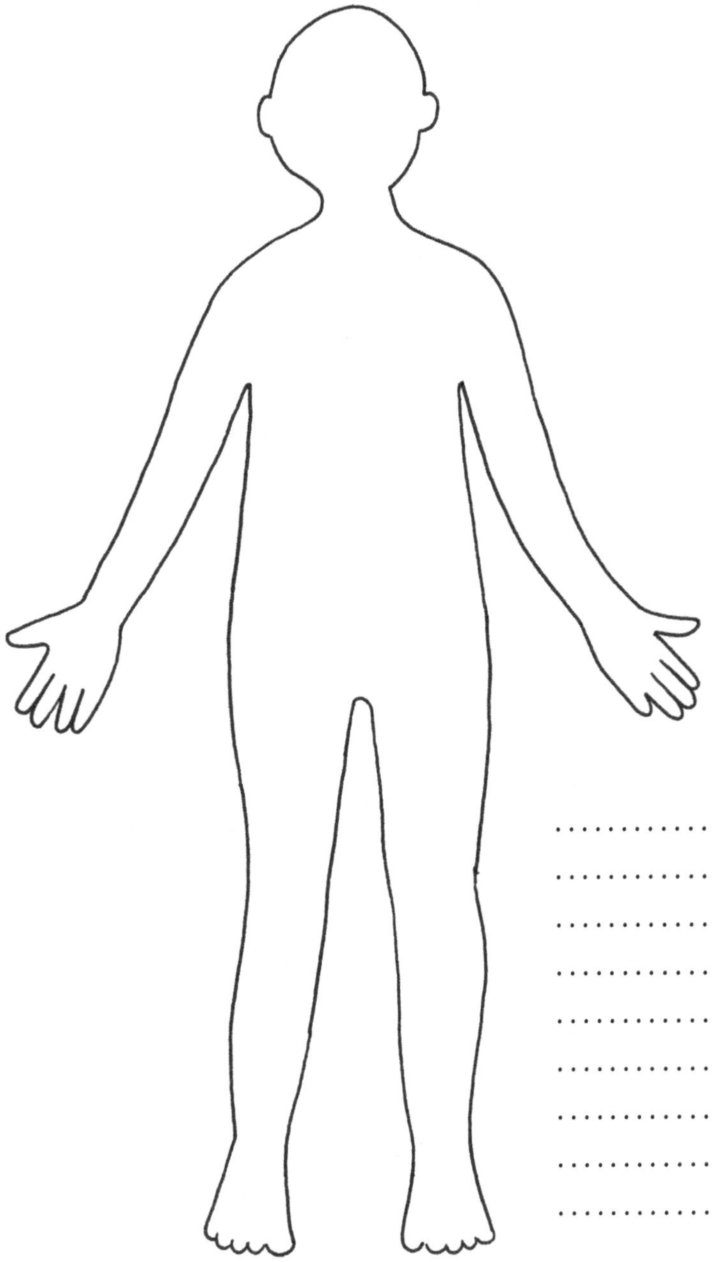

Mind
What is the story you tell yourself about why these losses happened to you?

Heart
What feelings and emotions are connected to these losses?

Body
Where do you feel these emotions in your body and how does your body react?

....

....

....

....

....

....

....

....

....

my mind, heart and body belong to me!

CORE LOSSES AND MY MIND

We are all living the story of our lives. You have a very smart brain that is actively trying to make sense of your history and journey. Your mind is doing the work of understanding and explaining why and how things happen to you. Write the story of why and how your core losses happened to you.

my MIND is amazing, strong and resilient!

CORE LOSSES AND MY HEART

Use colors, words and images to fill your heart with all of the feelings, thoughts, beliefs and emotions you have connected to your core losses.

MY HEART feels deeply and powerfully!

MY ATTACHMENT QUESTIONNAIRE

Describe what it's been like growing up in your family.

....

....

....

....

Describe your relationship with your parents as a young child. Begin as far back as you can remember.

....

....

....

....

List five adjectives or words that describe your relationship with your mother/caregiver starting from as far back as you can remember.

1. ....
2. ....
3. ....
4. ....
5. ....

Give an example for each adjective you chose from your memory of your childhood with your mother.

1. ....
   ....
2. ....
   ....
3. ....
   ....
4. ....
   ....
5. ....
   ....

List five adjectives or words that describe your relationship with your father/caregiver starting from as far back as you can remember.

1. ....

2. ....

3. ....

4. ....

5. ....

Give an example for each adjective you chose from your memory of your childhood with your father.

1. ....

....

2. ....

....

3. ....

....

4. ....

....

5. ....

....

When you were upset as a child, what would you do, and what would happen?

....

....

....

Were you ever afraid or terrified of a parent or caregiver? If yes, why?

....

....

....

When you were sick, injured or emotionally distressed, what would happen?

....

....

....

Why do you think your parents behaved the way they did during your childhood?

....

....

....

As a child, why did you think you were adopted or in foster care?

....

....

....

As a child, what were the thoughts and feelings you had about your birth/first mother and your birth/first father?

....

....

....

How did the experience of losing your birth/first parents impact your ability to attach and connect to, love and trust your current parents? What's been easy and what's been hard?

....

....

....

What are the strengths and unique characteristics that you bring to your family?

....

....

....

Learning the dance of attachment and connection takes time!
Go easy on yourself as you explore your history of loss or trauma!

— Chapter 2 —

REJECTION

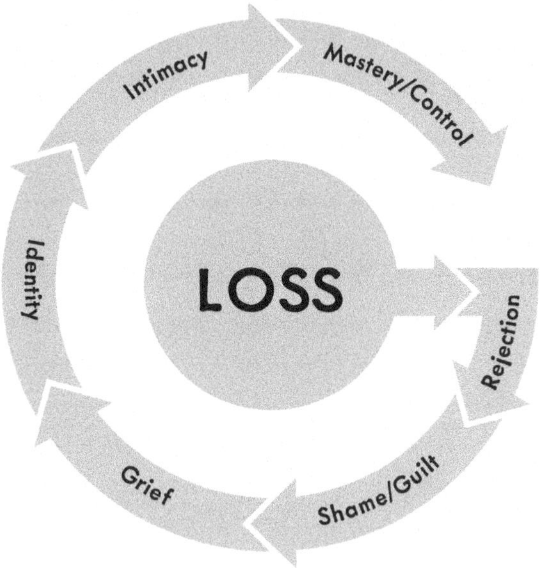

Rejection is the first spoke in the wheel coming from the Core Issue of loss.

When attachments to our birth/first parents and family are severed or lost, you may feel rejected, abandoned or unwanted. You may ask yourself, 'Why me?' and 'What did I do or not do to deserve this?' You may believe it's your fault, that you did something wrong or bad to create the loss and rejection.

You may find yourself fearing more rejection and abandonment. It may be hard to get close to others for fear of more rejection.

You may have built defensive walls around your heart to protect yourself from more rejection and loss. Draw or write what your defensive wall of protection looks like.

CIRCLES OF BELONGING

Our most important need is our need to belong, to feel meaningfully connected to those we love and care about. We need to know and to feel that we belong, that we are valued, needed and connected. Complete the Circles of Belonging by putting the names, groups and places where you feel a sense of belonging.

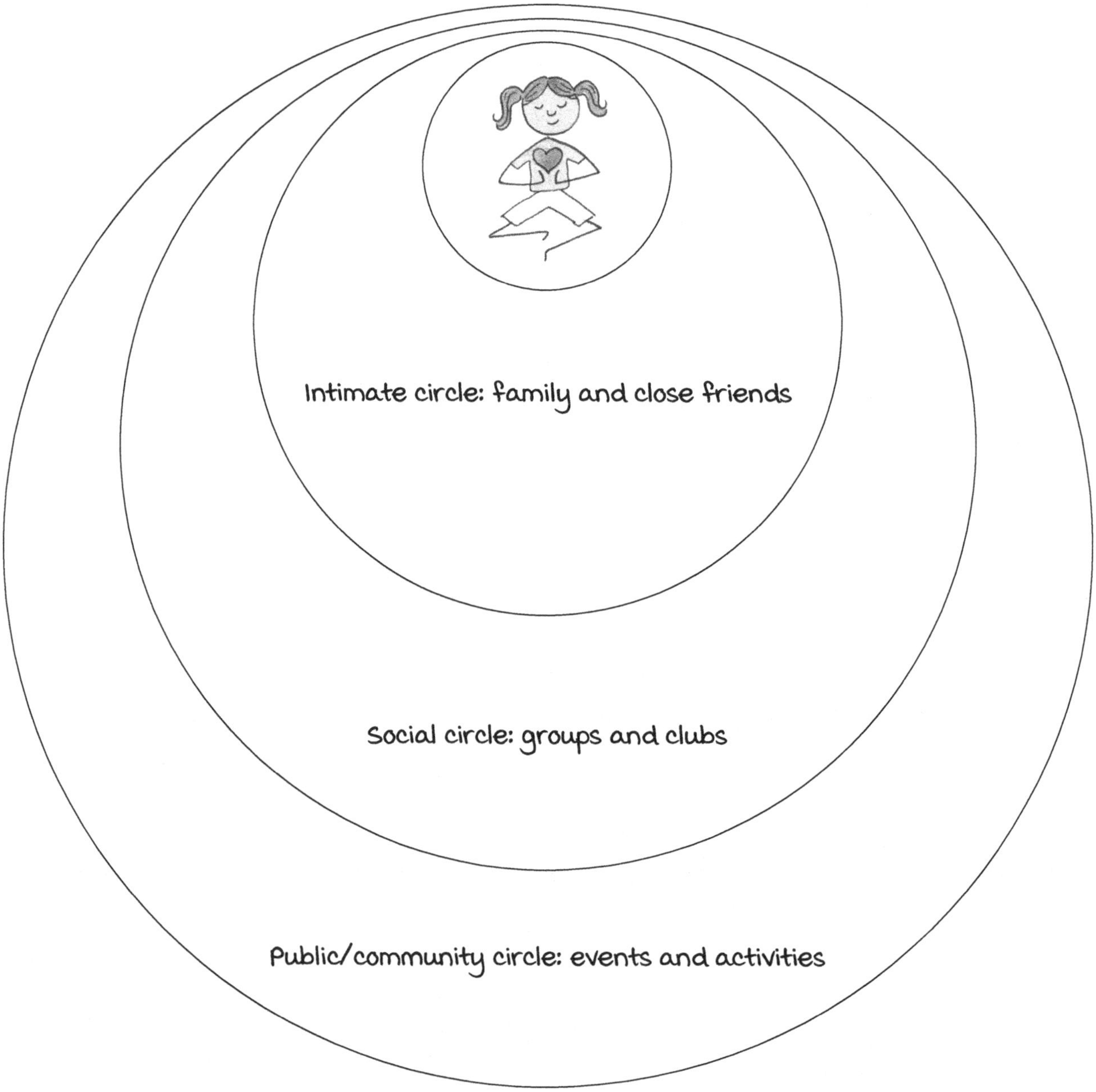

I deserve loving connections just like everyone else!

REJECTION AND MY EMOTIONS

The experience of rejection may trigger many different emotions. Think about a time you experienced rejection and use the emotion color wheel below to identify all the feelings you felt both during and after the experience of rejection.

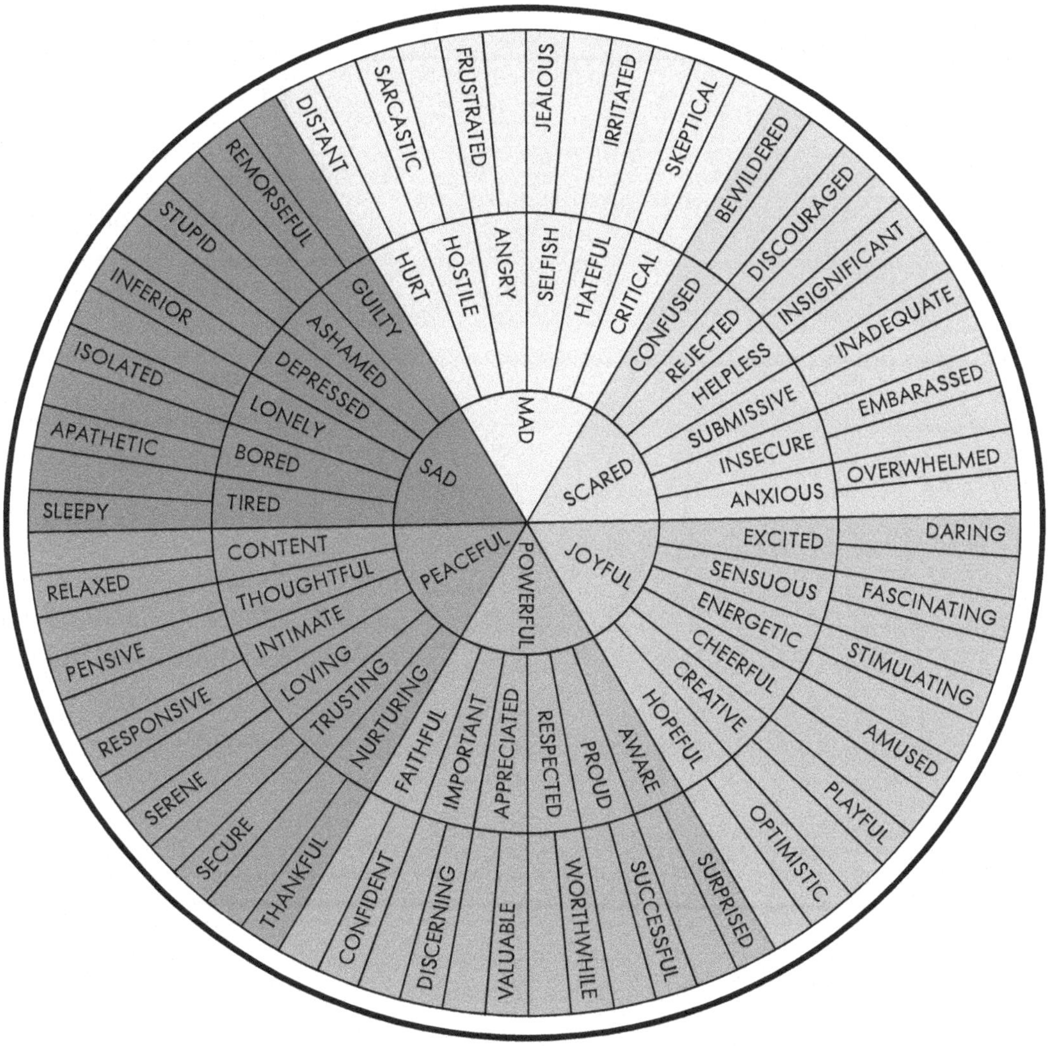

I'm built to feel deep emotions!
my feelings help me understand myself, my relationships and my world!

REJECTION IMPACTS THE MIND, HEART AND BODY

Rejection can be real, imagined or implied. The pain of being rejected is not so different from the pain of a physical injury; the depth of the pain is influenced by the closeness of the connection. Rejection is experienced in the mind, heart and body. It causes us to have trouble thinking clearly or being able to make good choices for ourselves. Choose one experience of rejection and answer the questions below.

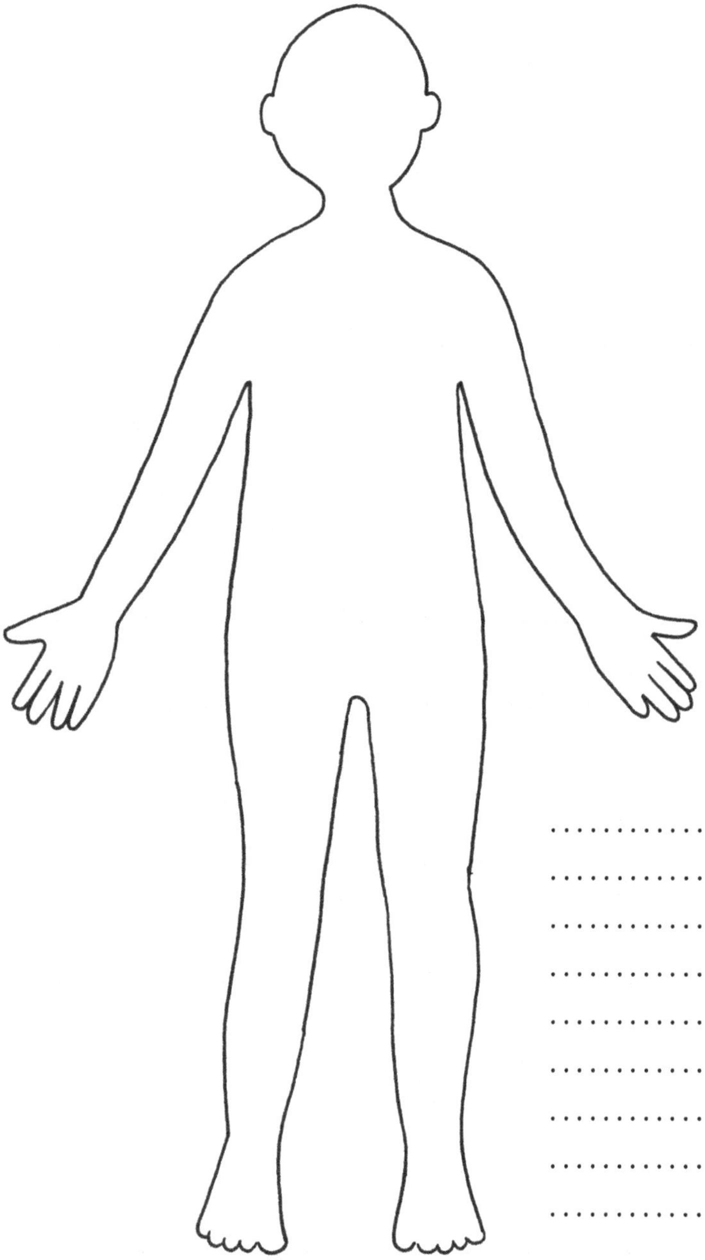

Mind
Our thoughts create feelings. What thoughts about yourself and others did you have?

Heart
What feelings did your thoughts trigger?

Body
Where in your body did you feel those emotions? What physical symptoms did you experience?

my mind, heart and body are learning and growing stronger each day!

REJECTION: WORDS MATTER!

It's easy to fall into the 'rejection trap' inside our own heads. The thoughts, beliefs and stories that we tell ourselves can be loaded with themes of rejection, real or imagined! Practice the below activity to use your words wisely and learn NOT to fall into the 'rejection trap'!

Words

matter

INSTEAD OF THIS	TRY THIS!
I'm not good enough.	I'm growing and learning every day. My mistakes help me grow.
The bad things that happened to me are my fault. I'm a mistake.	Yes, bad things happened to me. Those 'things' that happened don't define me; they are NOT who I am. I am so much more than the bad things that have happened to me.
No one really loves or cares about me.	There are people in my past, present and future who love and care about me.
I'm a failure. I'm stupid. I'm worthless. I'm bad.	I am good. I am strong. I am resilient. I am valuable. I am loveable.
I can't do anything right. I'll never be good at anything.	I have learned and grown a lot. I'm allowed to make mistakes like everyone else. There are so many things I want to learn and do.
I'm broken or damaged.	I'm healing, learning and growing.
I hate my body or how I look.	I'm thankful for my strong and resilient body. My body helps me feel, heal and experience the world.

When I change my thoughts, I change my world!

EARLY ATTACHMENT MATTERS!

The myth that babies and small children don't remember what happens to them led parents and professionals to underestimate the lingering effects of neglect, early trauma and attachment disruptions on the developing baby and their brain. Too much toxic stress is bad for little brains and bodies. The result can be too much fear, pain, suffering and distress, without enough love, safety, connection, joy and comfort.

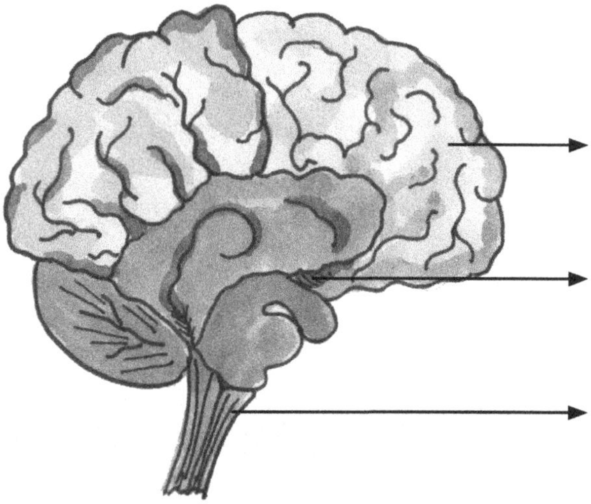

The good news is that the teen brain is going through a lot of changes. Your brain is still under construction! In fact, your brain can adapt, change and heal more quickly than an adult brain.

It's important to know that our bodies and brains remember everything, both consciously and unconsciously. When young brains have experienced a lot of painful, hurtful and scary things, memories and feelings get stored in our Limbic System. A smell, a sound, a dream or a memory can trigger the intense emotions connected to those old experiences.

Here are some things that can help you identify, express and release some of the painful emotions that may be stored in your Limbic System:

- Take five minutes each day, close your eyes, take slow deep breaths, allow your body to be still and notice any sensations.
- Start a Feelings Journal. At the end of the day, write down all the different emotions you experience throughout the day. Don't judge yourself. Just try and observe yourself and take note of any emotional themes.
- In a safe place, create a Feelings Chair, where any and all emotions are OK and allowed to be validated, expressed and released.
- Write a poem, letter or song that expresses a painful memory or trigger.

my brain and body is built to heal!

WHAT TO DO WITH ALL THAT STRESS

We experience STRESS through our senses (body).

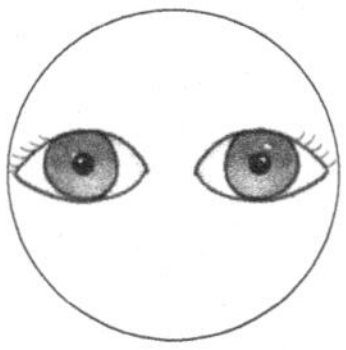 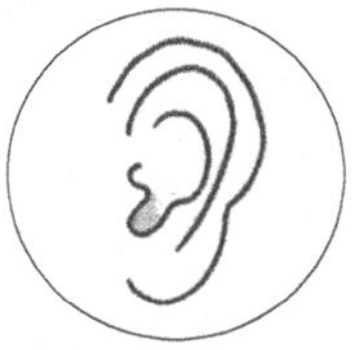 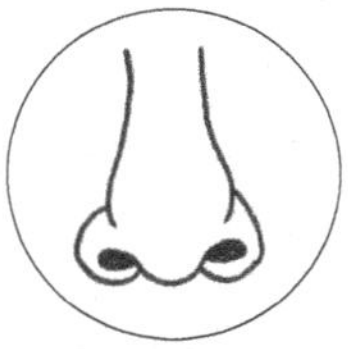  

Did you know that there is 'good stress' and 'bad stress'? From the moment we enter the world, we are learning how to cope with 'good stress', and it is an important part of healthy human development. All babies and children have developmental milestones that require them to learn something new all the time. We need to learn to crawl, walk, run, talk, read, write, and so on, and as we grow and develop the learning becomes more complex. We feel smart and strong when we're learning from 'good stress'.

'Bad' or 'toxic stress' refers to the body's response to too much stress. When we experience toxic stress our heart rate increases, our blood pressure goes up and stress hormones are activated, which triggers a fight/flight/freeze response. The difference between toxic stress and good stress depends on how quickly we return to feeling calm and grounded. Too much toxic stress shifts our energy away from learning and growth, towards survival and safety. It can rob us of feeling joy, love, connection and laughter.

Babies and children are dependent on their parents and caregivers to help their brains and bodies reduce toxic stress. Parental attachment plays a critical role in teaching children how to identify and regulate their emotions. Self-regulation skills are most easily learned when children experience 'good stress', which requires supportive, loving caregivers who can help their child feel safe and secure while minimizing feelings of isolation, fear, worthlessness and despair.

To reduce toxic stress, become aware of your senses: what you see, what you hear, what you smell, what you touch and FEEL. We experience stress through our senses and body. For example, loud noises, people yelling, chaos or clutter, lack of structure, dogs barking can feel overwhelming and trigger a stress response, while certain pleasurable odors may trigger a calming or soothing response, like baking cookies or essential oils like lavender. Listening to the sounds of the ocean, or rain, or rhythmic music feels calming and relaxing, which helps to detox our senses and body.

De-stressing tips (for teens and their parents)

- Teens need to FEEL safe and secure. They need to feel secure, knowing their parents can take care of them and meet their needs no matter what else is going on in the adults' lives. None of us can feel safe and secure by ourselves all the time; humans are wired to be in relationship with one another in order to feel safe and secure. Feelings of safety and security are rooted in permanent attachment relationships.
- Exercise. Our bodies need to be 'in motion' to de-stress, so be creative and get your body moving. When we are in a fearful or anxious state, we are in a heightened state of arousal or alarm, relying on lower-functioning brain regions. Walking, running, dancing, singing, swimming, hiking,

yoga, deep breathing all use brain stem-related somatosensory networks which calm the body and brain.

- Structure your day. We feel better when our world is predictable and stable. Create daily 'together time' by having family meals, or a time when we can share the highs and lows from our day. Teens are more resilient when stress occurs if they have predictable relationships and routines when life gets stressful. Teens who have experienced years of toxic stress need more time to learn emotional regulation skills.
- Play and be silly! Play is probably the most effective stress reducer. It gives us an outlet for the physical energy that toxic stress creates. Play creates opportunities for joy, laughter and silliness. When we play, we replace stress hormones with pleasurable hormones that allow us to feel happy, connected and loved.
- Take a sensory break. Give yourself a sensory break. Allow all your senses to go on 'shutdown'; be quiet, calm and still. Limit screens and media. The mind cannot calm down inside a body filled with toxic stress. Try music, drawing, meditation, yoga, coloring, prayer, walking, reading, and so on.
- Learn the 'language of emotion'. We are built to feel! Learn the language of emotion by learning to identify and express all your feelings. Your emotions are giving you important information about what you need. Listening to your feelings will help you learn more about yourself and what you need from the people who care about you.

Learning to de-stress your body and mind takes practice!

GOOD STRESS VS BAD STRESS

When children and teens experience bad or toxic stress the body, heart and brain are working overtime and struggling just to survive. When you experience toxic stress your heart rate increases, your blood pressure goes up, stress hormones are activated, all of which triggers a fight/flight/freeze response. It's important to help the body and mind learn to relax, de-stress and find inner calm. Write down ten things YOU can do to de-stress your body and mind. Practice one or two EVERY day!

Ten things I do to de-stress my body and mind

1. ....
....
2. ....
....
3. ....
....
4. ....
....
5. ....
....
6. ....
....
7. ....
....
8. ....
....
9. ....
....
10. ....
....
11. ....
....

I deserve to feel calm, grounded and relaxed.

MY SENSORY TRIGGERS

Teens who have a history of attachment disruptions, trauma and neglect have experienced those events through all five of their senses. It's important to know that your body and brain remember everything. Your body and brain are strong, resilient and ready to heal. You have already survived the hardest parts of your past. Healing occurs when you learn to express and release any unprocessed pain and trauma. It is absolutely possible to triumph over your trauma!

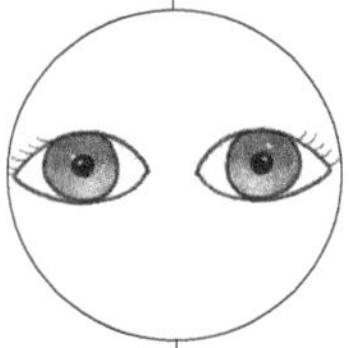

My eyes help me see and understand my world and life. I may have bad memories about the difficult things I've seen.

When I see these things, I get upset, anxious or triggered:

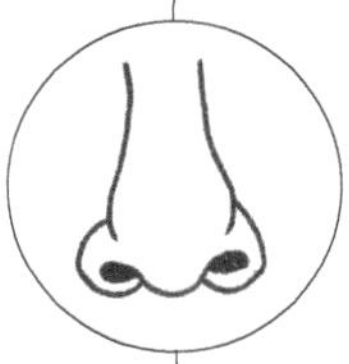

My olfactory system (smell) is wired to my feeling brain. Certain smells trigger strong emotions, either positively or negatively.

These are the smells I love:

These are the smells that I strongly dislike or that trigger me:

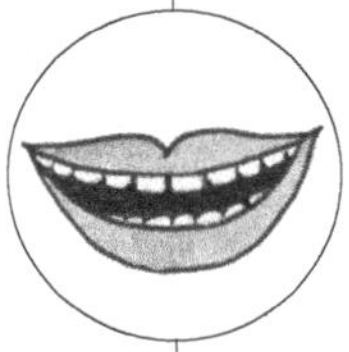

My sense of taste has been developing since I was a baby. Early neglect or abuse can cause food issues, like over-eating, under-eating, binge eating or hoarding.

I have these kinds of challenges connected to food or eating:

My body, skin and sense of touch are always helping me to process and understand my world.

I like to receive these kinds of touch and affection:

I don't like to receive these kinds of touch and affection:

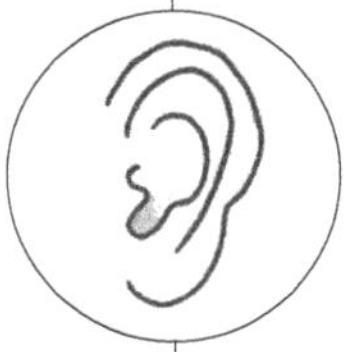

My ears help me listen, understand, and remember sounds, words and voices.

I like these kinds of sounds:

I don't like these kinds of sounds:

my senses are amazing—they help me understand everything in my world!

REJECTION HURTS!

Feeling rejected hurts! When you think or perceive that you are being rejected your thoughts and beliefs will trigger certain feelings. Understanding your thoughts and feelings about rejection will help you make positive and healthy decisions about your actions and behaviors. If you experienced a lot of rejection as a child and teen, exploring your beliefs and feelings can feel empowering and healing. Complete the following activity to understand your own Cycle of Rejection.

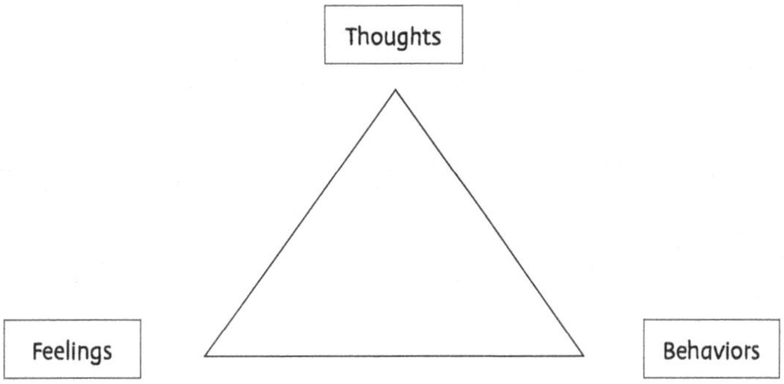

Something stressful happens and I think I'm being rejected. I begin to tell myself things like .... and .... and .... and .... and ....

These thoughts that I'm thinking create the following feelings:

1. .... 4. ....

2. .... 5. ....

3. .... 6. ....

As a result of my thoughts and feelings about *rejection*, I act or behave in the following ways:

....

....

Your thoughts and beliefs have the power to impact your emotions and actions. When you 'think' or 'perceive' that you are being rejected, here are some healthy and positive things you can do:

1. Be curious! Question whether your thoughts and perceptions about the situation are accurate. Sometimes old patterns of rejection can resurface. Find out the facts!
2. Go get some exercise! When we feel rejected, the pain centers in our brain and body get triggered. Walk, run, hike, shoot hoops, play soccer, do yoga, MOVE your body!

Changing patterns of rejection into patterns of CONNECTION helps me heal and thrive!

REJECTION IN ADOPTION AND FOSTER CARE

Teens who have experienced foster care, kinship and adoption can experience rejection in different ways. They 'may' feel rejected or abandoned by their birth/first parents or former foster parents or their adoptive or kinship parents. Complete the grid below to explore where 'feelings of rejection' or 'fears of being rejected' happen to you.

Relationship to you	**What happened?**	**How did you feel?**	**How did you cope?**
Birth/first parents			
Extended birth family; grandparents, aunts/ uncles, cousins			
Foster parents (Do one for each foster parent)			
Adoptive or kinship parents			
Siblings or other important connections			

My story belongs to me! Only I know how it feels to be me!

MANAGING MY EMOTIONAL TRIGGERS

We all have automatic thought patterns that are triggered when we're upset, hurt or angry. Understanding your own thought patterns is the first step in making sure that your 'inner dialogue' is helping YOU find internal balance and to bounce back from a stressful event. Taking good care of yourself begins with making sure your mind is your best friend!

Thoughts	**Feelings**	**Actions**
When I'm upset, hurt or angry, these are the automatic thoughts I have:	When I'm upset, hurt or angry, these are my feelings connected to my automatic thoughts:	When I'm upset, hurt or angry, my automatic thoughts trigger more negative actions and behaviors such as: ....
Next time I'm upset, hurt or angry I can use these thoughts that are focused on my strengths to find balance, calm and self-awareness:	Next time I'm upset, hurt or angry these are the feelings I would have if I replaced my old automatic thoughts with ones that were focused on my strengths:	Next time I'm upset, hurt or angry I can use thoughts focused on my strengths that help me find balance and calm. Then I can act and behave in a way that helps me feel understood and good about myself: ....

It's OK to feel. It's OK to release old hurt feelings of pain, loss and rejection. Healing from my past takes time!

DEAR ADOPTION OR FOSTER CARE

There are positive and negative things about adoption and foster care. Most people like to hear only about the positive things. Now that you are a teen, you will understand much more about what you lost and how hard being adopted or in foster care can be sometimes. Being adopted or in foster care will have had a big impact on your life. You need to be allowed to express ALL your thoughts, beliefs and feelings, so use the space below to explain these.

Dear Adoption or Foster Care,

my story is mine to tell. I decide who gets to know me and my story!

DEAR BIRTH OR FIRST MOTHER

You will have had a lot of thoughts, feelings and questions about your birth mother. This letter will help you be completely honest about everything as you spend some time exploring what's inside your own heart and mind about them. Even if they never read this letter, you need to be allowed to explore and express everything you think and feel.

Dear Birth/First Mother,

Sometimes my journey feels really hard! I'm learning to go easy on myself as I practice taking good care of my mind, heart and body!

DEAR BIRTH OR FIRST FATHER

You will have had a lot of thoughts, feelings and questions about your birth father. This letter will help you be completely honest about everything as you spend some time exploring what's inside your own heart and mind about them. Even if they never read this letter, you need to be allowed to explore and express everything you think and feel.

Dear Birth/First Father,

I am building 'emotional muscle' and strength each time I explore and express the hard parts of my story.

— Chapter 3 —

SHAME AND GUILT

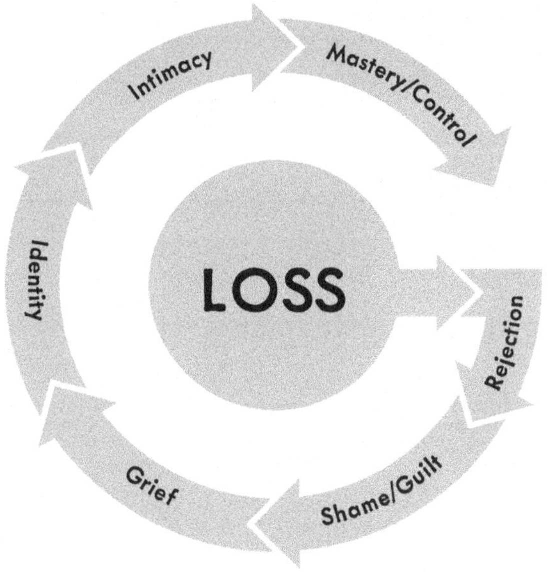

The second spoke in the wheel of the Seven Core Issues is shame and guilt.

Guilt is about 'What I did'. If we do something wrong, guilt motivates us to fix the problem, or say 'I'm sorry', or make amends.

Shame is about 'Who I am'. Shame makes us feel bad, worthless or 'less than'. Shame can come from early trauma, loss, abandonment, abuse or neglect.

Shame makes us feel small and powerless, as if we want to disappear, avoid eye contact or collapse inward. Shame makes us feel as if our core self is 'bad' or 'damaged'.

Try this:

- I am NOT what happened to me!
- Trauma is NOT 'Who I am'; trauma is something that happened to me.
- I am so much more. My brain, body, spirit and self are mine!
- I am actively creating the 'ME' I want to be.
- I get to choose and decide the 'ME' I will become.

I am the expert about ME. I love these things about ME:

....

....

....

LIKING MYSELF

Some of us grew up with critical or negative messages about ourselves. We may struggle to see ourselves in a positive light or even like ourselves. Practice focusing on your positive and likeable qualities.

My name is ....

I am .... years old and am unique and intelligent.

I'm really interested in quite a few things:

....

....

....

I also have learned a lot while I've been here on the planet. Here are some of the positive things that I've learned about myself:

....

....

....

Here are some things that I'm really good at:

....

....

....

My favorite things to do in my spare time are:

....

....

....

I also know that no one is perfect and I make mistakes. These are some things I'm not very good at:

....

....

....

I also like to learn about new things. These are some things I'm interested in learning more about:

Over the years, others have told me they like the following things about me:

These are the things that I like most about myself:

I am unique! There is only one amazing me in this whole wide world! I am growing and learning every day! I get to decide the me I will become!

DE-SHAMING MY MIND

We all have an inner voice. Some of us have internalized a lot of negative or shaming messages about ourselves. These negative and hurtful thoughts get in the way of us feeling happy and positive about our life and accomplishments. To de-shame your mind, you need to get rid of the hurtful and negative messages you say to yourself. Put the shaming and negative thoughts about yourself in the trash can below.

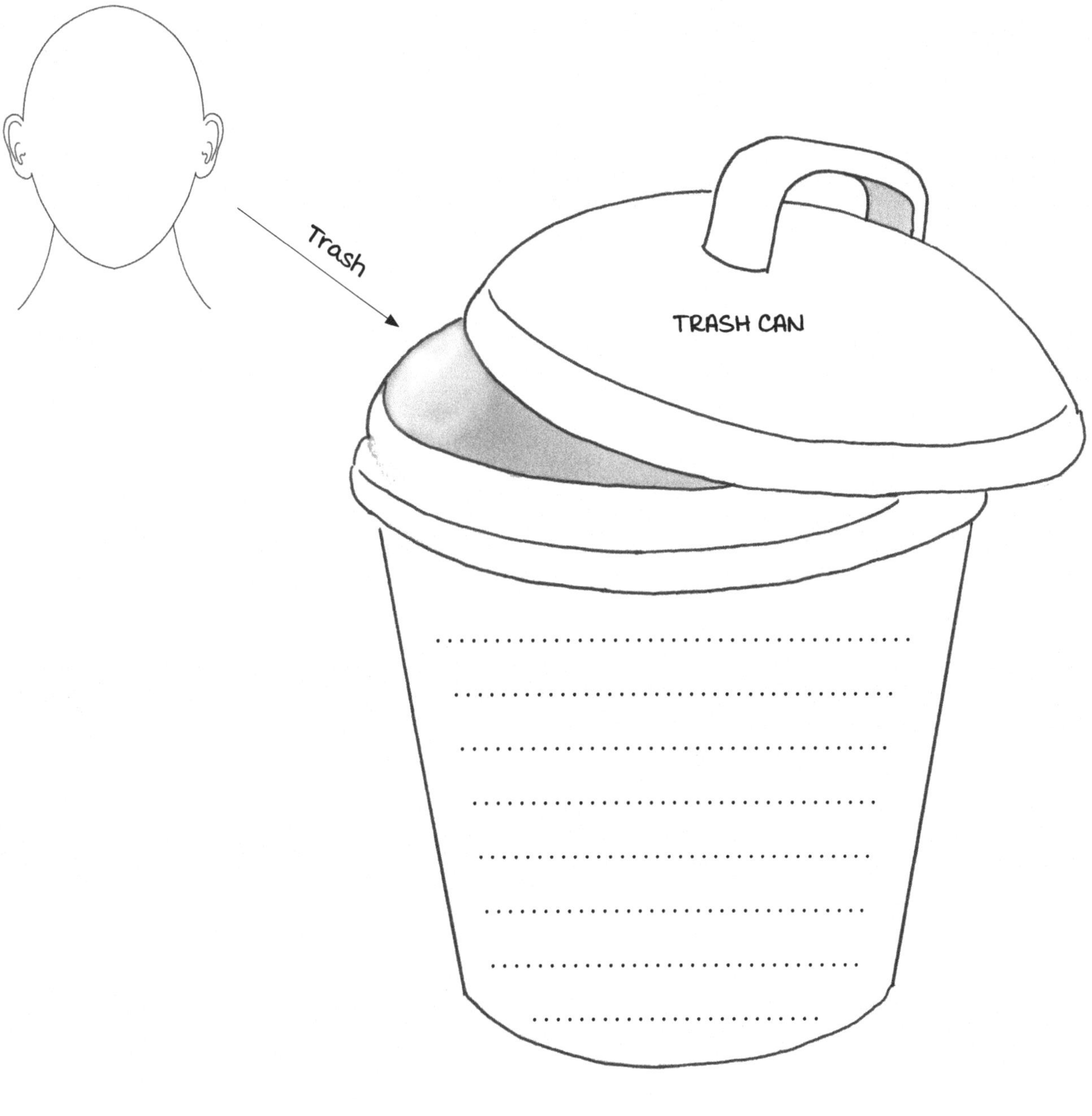

I've been through enough hard stuff. I'm done being mean to myself inside my own mind!

PRACTICING SELF-ACCEPTANCE

Mirror, mirror on the wall, I'm saying these positive messages to myself so I can learn to love and accept myself! I'm doing the best I can. When I know better, I do better. When I feel better, I do better.

List and then recite five positive messages of encouragement to YOURSELF each day.

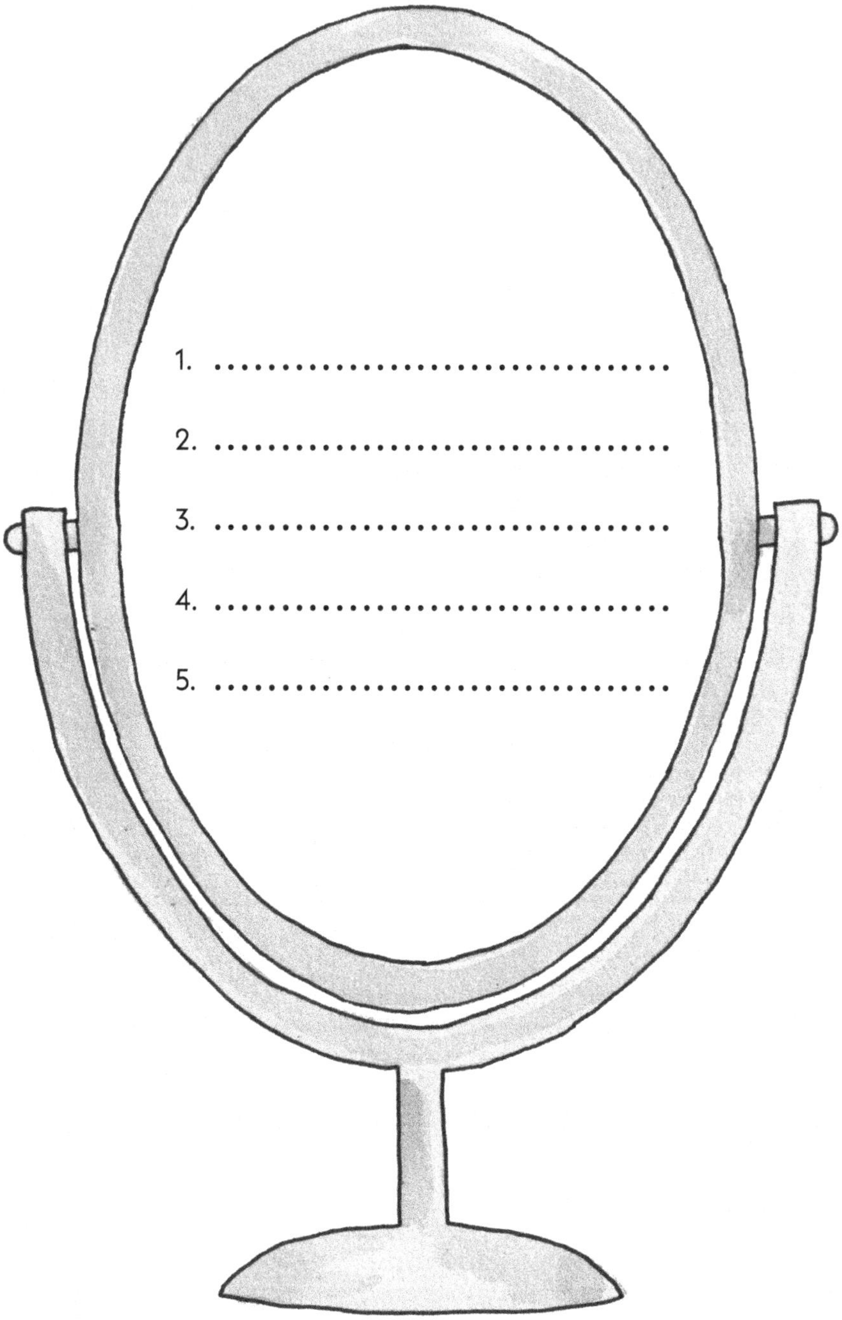

I accept myself and all the things that make me uniquely me.

SECRETS VS PRIVACY

There is a long history in adoption and foster care of misinformation, limited information and not telling children the truth about their story and history. Sometimes parents and caregivers withhold facts or information to protect their child from pain and loss.

As a teen, it's important to know the truth and facts about your story so YOU can 1) understand why you were in foster care or adopted; 2) grieve, heal and process all the feelings connected to this experience; 3) have all the pieces of your puzzle so you can build a strong identity or sense of self.

- Secrets create mistrust.
- Secrets create fantasies as we try and fill in missing pieces of our story.
- Secrets create feelings of shame, guilt, anxiety and fear.
- Secrets create confusion and make building an identity difficult.

Your personal story and narrative belongs to YOU. The story you tell yourself about who you are and why certain things happened should be based on truthful and factual information. And since your story belongs to YOU, only you can decide how much of your story you want to share. Privacy means taking control of your personal story and intentionally sharing the parts you decide you want to share.

Not having these parts of my story has been painful or stressful for me:

....

....

....

This is how I see the difference between privacy and 'keeping secrets':

....

....

....

Sometimes when children move too many times and have too many changes in their parents or caregivers, parts of their story get lost. Sometimes teens want to search and reconnect with people they cared about and lost to find some of the missing parts of their story and life. Here is what has happened to me and what kinds of things I am searching for:

....

....

....

I'm comfortable sharing these parts of my adoption or foster care story:

....

....

....

I'm uncomfortable sharing these parts of my adoption or foster care story:

....

....

....

My story belongs to me. Sometimes I will choose to share my story and other times I may choose not to share at all. Telling my story in a way that feels authentic and empowering to me is important. These are some of the things I think about when I'm deciding how much of my story to share and with whom:

....

....

....

Feeling good about myself and who I am is always important. When I share parts of my story or who I am with other people, I can use these words that reflect my strengths, passions, values and core beliefs:

....

....

....

....

....

....

....

....

....

....

....

....

....

....

It's my story! I decide how much of my story I can trust others to know!

ALL THE PIECES OF ME

One of the hardest parts about being adopted or in foster care is being disconnected from the parents and family tree that made you. Those parents and those two family trees hold pieces of your story, heritage and identity. It can feel overwhelming, confusing or hurtful at times to feel as if you don't have all the pieces to your own history or identity.

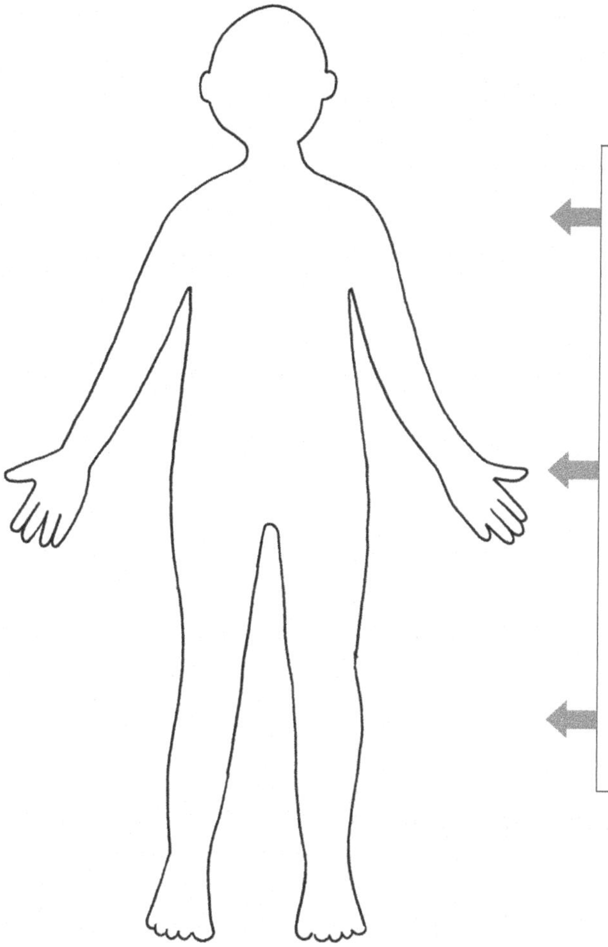

- My body image, size, shape and appearance. Who do I look like? Where do I get my physical traits?
- What is the story of my birth/first mother? What was her childhood and life like? Who is she? My story begins with her story!
- What is the story of my birth/first father? What was his childhood and life like? Who is he? Does he know about me?
- What is the culture/ethnicity and race of my birth/first parents? How am I like them? How am I not like them? Did they have more kids?

As a teen, it's my job to figure out who I am and what I want to do with my life. These are the missing pieces I'm still struggling to learn and understand:

....

....

....

I have more puzzle pieces than most other teens. I'm learning to go easy on myself—having all these missing pieces can feel hard sometimes!

ADVERSE CHILDHOOD EXPERIENCES

For teens, knowing and understanding your ACE score gives you the ability to have compassion for your 'younger self' that survived trauma, neglect, a parent's mental illness or addiction, or moving a lot in foster care, and so on. Knowing your ACE score helps you understand why you may struggle with certain feelings like sadness, anger, depression, shame, guilt, anxiety or loneliness.

Toxic stress occurs when we are exposed to *overwhelming* amounts of fear and distress due to violence, threats of violence, physical or sexual abuse, parental loss or abandonment, foster care, parental addiction and/or mental illness. Trauma is something that 'happens' to us. It does NOT define who we are! Healing the heart, mind and body is always possible! Draw or write the difficult things that happened to you at the different stages of your life.

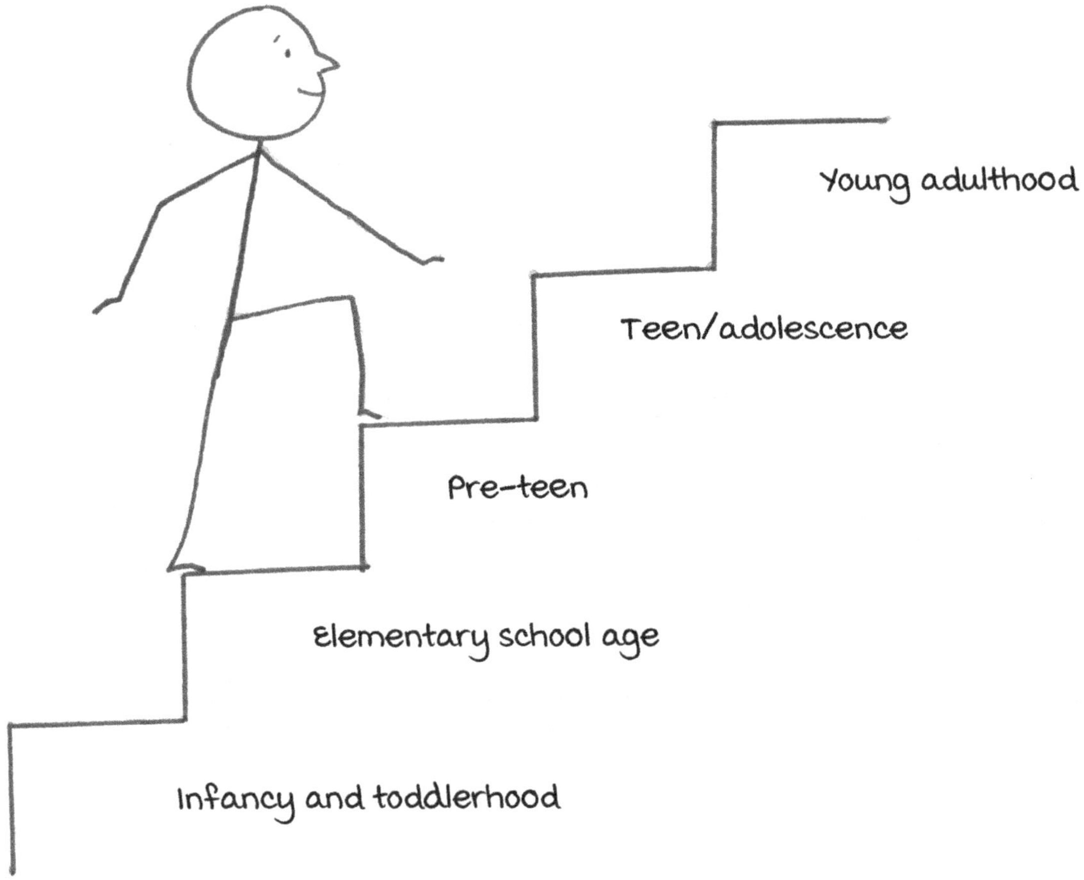

I AM in charge of ME and all the different parts of my healing journey!

FINDING YOUR ACE SCORE

While you were growing up, during your first 18 years of life:

1. Did a parent or other adult in the household often swear at you, insult you, put you down/or humiliate you? Or act in a way that made you afraid that you might be physically hurt?

   Yes No

   If yes enter 1 ....

2. Did a parent or other adult in the household often push, grab, slap, or throw something at you? Or ever hit you so hard that you had marks or were injured?

   Yes No

   If yes enter 1 ....

3. Did an adult or person at least five years older than you ever touch or fondle you or have you touch their body in a sexual way? Or try to or actually have oral, anal or vaginal sex with you?

   Yes No

   If yes enter 1 ....

4. Did you often feel that no one in your family loved you or thought you were important, or your family didn't look out for each other, feel close to each other or support each other?

   Yes No

   If yes enter 1 ....

5. Did you often feel that you didn't have enough to eat, had to wear dirty clothes or had no one to protect you? Or your parents were too drunk/high to take care of you or take you to the doctor?

   Yes No

   If yes enter 1 ....

6. Were your parents ever separated or divorced or did they leave you?

   Yes No

   If yes enter 1 ....

7. Was your mother or stepmother: Often pushed, grabbed, slapped, or had something thrown at her? Or sometimes or often kicked, bitten, hit with a fist, or hit with something hard? Or ever repeatedly hit or threatened with a gun or knife?

   Yes No

   If yes enter 1 ....

8. Did you live with anyone who was a problem drinker or alcoholic or who used drugs?

   Yes No

   If yes enter 1 ....

9. Was a household member depressed or mentally ill or did a household member attempt suicide?

   Yes No

   If yes enter 1 ....

10. Did a household member go to prison?

   Yes No

   If yes enter 1 ....

Now go to https://acestoohigh.com to learn more about your score and tools to help cope and heal.

my body, heart and mind ALWAYS want to grow, learn and heal.

MY ACE STORY

When bad things happen to us as children, it may be hard to talk about because it's easy to get overwhelmed or flooded by the feelings connected to those memories. It is important to tell the story of what happened to us as children because early trauma is never the fault of the child. Sometimes children blame themselves for the bad things that happen to them. Telling the facts of your story, now that you're older and more resilient, may help to relieve lingering guilt, shame, hurt or self-blame.

When I was younger, I remember a time when something bad happened to me:

....

....

....

....

First:

....

....

....

....

Next, I remember:

....

....

....

....

Last, I remember:

....

....

....

....

I remember feeling:

....

....

....

....

When I think about that memory now, I feel:

....

....

....

....

These are the things that I did in order to survive and cope:

....

....

....

....

These are the things I do now to feel safe, secure and grounded:

....

....

....

....

These are the people in life who support me to heal and thrive:

....

....

....

....

Now when I get upset, hurt or triggered, I can use these healthy coping strategies:

....

....

....

....

Learning survival skills kept me alive and safe! Learning to heal and thrive is what my body, heart and mind need now!

TYPES OF ABUSE AND TRAUMA

Check all that apply to you:

- ☐ Physical abuse: being physically hit, kicked, punched, pushed, bitten.
- ☐ Childhood neglect: when a parent or caregiver fails to provide adequate food, shelter, clothing, medical care, education and proper care and supervision, or forces a child to do things inappropriate for their age.
- ☐ Emotional abuse: when a caregiver engages in a consistent pattern of demeaning, critical, shaming, threatening and rejecting behaviors that negatively impact a child's emotional development and sense of self-worth.
- ☐ Sexual abuse: any interaction with another person in which a child is used for the sexual stimulation of the abuser or perpetrator.
- ☐ Medical trauma and accidents: physical, emotional and psychological pain and suffering from accidents and/or medical events.
- ☐ Vicarious trauma: watching, witnessing and feeling the emotional pain while someone you care about is being beaten, molested or emotionally abused.
- ☐ Institutionalization or orphanage care: while these settings 'may' meet basic needs for food, safety and shelter, they cannot meet the primary attachment, emotional and developmental needs of a child.
- ☐ Bullying: a deliberate action with an intent to cause physical, emotional and psychological harm to someone viewed as different or less powerful.
- ☐ Intimate partner violence or 'domestic violence': occurs when a person intentionally causes harm or threatens to cause harm. Controlling and threatening behaviors include verbal and physical aggression, humiliation, shaming, terrorizing, stalking and intentional isolation from supportive relationships.
- ☐ Complex trauma: when a child has experienced multiple traumatic events that have been severe and prolonged, like chronic neglect for multiple years or experiencing rotating caregivers in foster care for multiple years, or having an abusive parent/caregiver.

Trauma symptoms get stuck in the body and mind. Exercise, play and be silly to release toxic stress!

TRAUMA AND YOUR BODY

What does trauma feel like in your body? Use the diagram to color in all the trauma symptoms you experience. Remember that taking good care of your body is the first step in healing from loss and trauma.

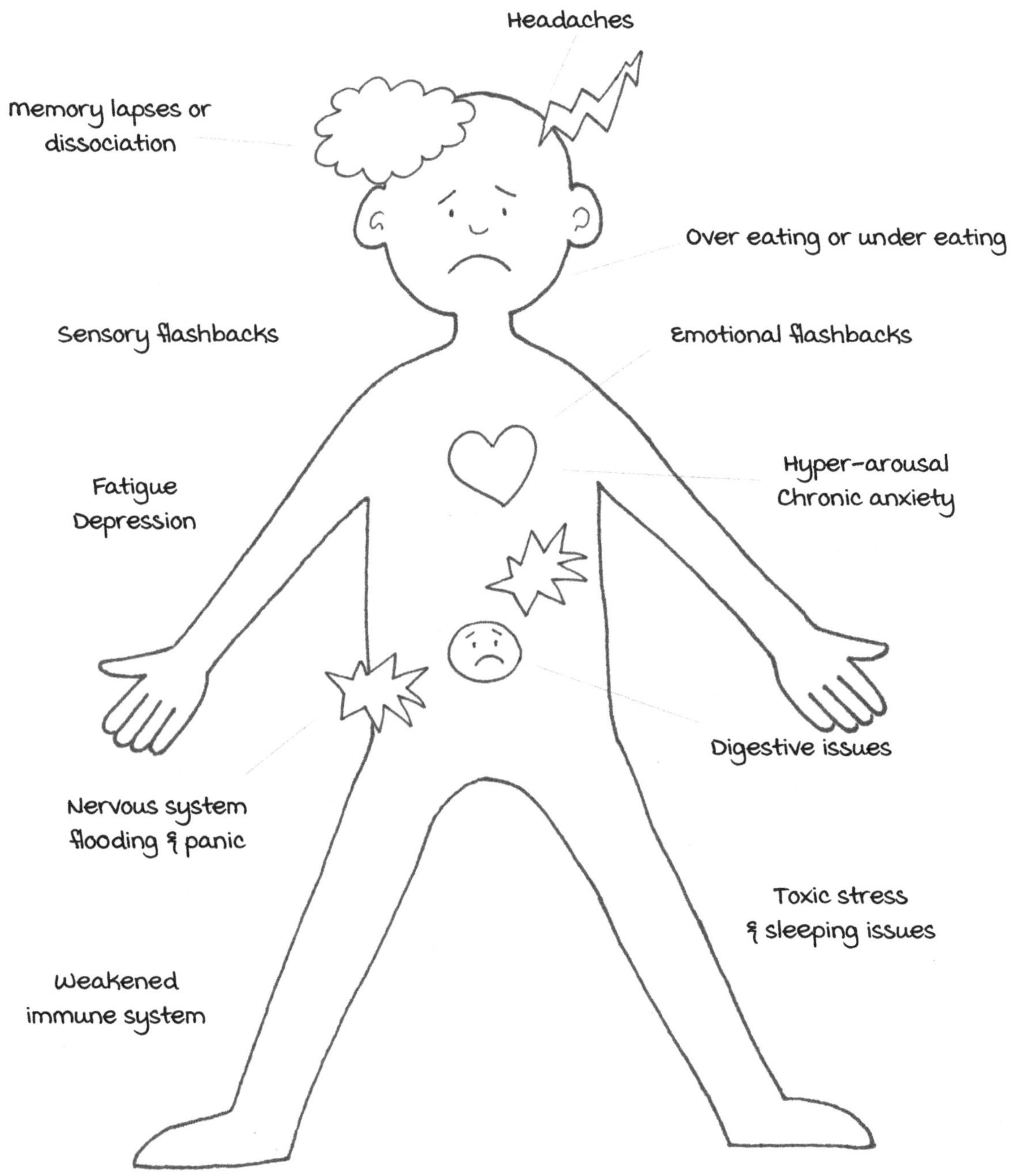

Listen to the wisdom in your body!

MY TRAUMA CHECKLIST

Experiencing different kinds of abuse, neglect, attachment disruptions and traumatic losses can be overwhelming and confusing sometimes. Use the self-reflection tool to help you understand your own trauma symptoms.

	Never	A little	A lot	Always
I feel irritable, stressed or frustrated.				
It's hard to concentrate, focus and learn.				
I have flashbacks or unwanted memories that trigger my body and emotions.				
I'm easily startled and feel as if something bad is about to happen.				
I feel bad or negative about myself.				
I work hard to repress or avoid my feelings and emotions.				
I don't enjoy doing pleasurable things, including the things I used to like doing.				
It's hard for me to trust others.				
I have nightmares or night terrors.				
I can overreact; I have a lot of intense feelings that get easily triggered.				
I feel disconnected from my body and emotions.				
I tend to over-eat or under-eat.				
I am anxious and nervous about most things.				
My body feels heavy, exhausted and fatigued.				
I feel as if things will only get worse for me.				
I feel as if I don't deserve to be loved or cared about.				
I try to never talk about my past.				
I feel like hurting myself.				
I have negative thoughts about my body and appearance.				
I feel lost and confused, as if I don't know who I am.				

Trauma is 'what happened' to me. It does not define who I am!

WHAT TO DO WITH ALL THAT TRAUMA

Remember that early neglect, toxic stress and trauma linger in the body, heart and mind. It's important to do things to help release the unprocessed experiences and feelings of fear, hurt, pain, shame, anger and despair that can lead to chronic anxiety and depression. Practice doing one of the following each day!

- Play a game and be silly on purpose.
- Watch a sad movie and let yourself cry.
- Go for a walk, hike, swim, bike, shoot hoops, play soccer, jog.
- Draw, paint or color a picture.
- Play music loudly and dance around your room.
- Write in a journal about things that are important to you.
- Build a fort and hang out with a friend.
- Watch funny cat (or dog) videos and laugh out loud.
- Practice yoga and learn to strengthen your body and mind.
- Breathe deeply and slowly for five minutes.
- Draw a picture of hurt, fear, trauma, anger, healing and love.
- Create a 'Feelings Space' in your room where ALL feelings are OK and all feelings get to be expressed, validated and released.
- Call someone who cares about you and talk about something meaningful.
- Visualize yourself floating on a cloud and allow each part of your body to relax and be still.
- Light a scented candle and enjoy the beautiful smell.
- Bake or cook something yummy and delicious.
- Take a bubble bath instead of a shower—relax and enjoy!
- Let your 'younger self' out to play. Play your favorite childhood game.
- Ask a friend to tell you all the things they like about YOU.
- Curl up in your favorite cozy blanket and watch your favorite movie.
- Cuddle with your pet.
- Say out loud, 'My body is safe, strong, resilient and ready to heal.'
- Wrap yourself up like a burrito or sleep with a weighted blanket.
- Take your shoes off and press your feet into the ground or grass.
- Chew bubble gum and blow big bubbles.

I let my body and heart be playful and silly so I can feel joy and happiness!

— Chapter 4 —

GRIEF

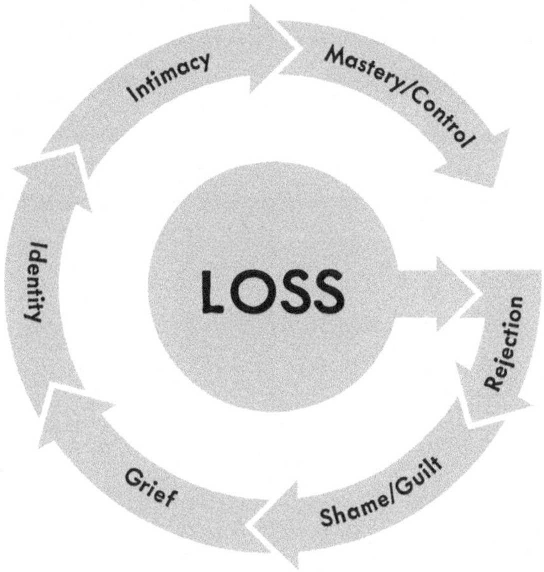

The third spoke in the Seven Core Issues wheel is grief. It's the pain, suffering and grief from all the losses and trauma connected to adoption, kinship and foster care.

For teens:

- Repressing, avoiding or denying intense emotions doesn't help address the deep pain, loss or trauma.
- Grief can often look like anger or constant agitation.
- Unacknowledged grief can turn into depression or chronic anxiety.
- Their bodies are built to feel: headaches, stomach aches, fatigue, sleep issues and food issues all are common symptoms of grief.
- Displaced grief, hurt and anger can be projected onto those they love.
- grief symptoms often intensify as they mature and understand the reality and complexity of what happened to them and how it impacted their life. Yes, even those adopted as infants.

Know this:

- So much of the loss and pain connected to adoption and foster care is unacknowledged and ungrieved. Non-adopted people, including parents and professionals, often minimize the pain, loss and trauma.
- YOU are the expert of your own journey.
- Healing from past loss and trauma is not only possible, it's empowering!

GRIEF IS MESSY AND I AM STRONG

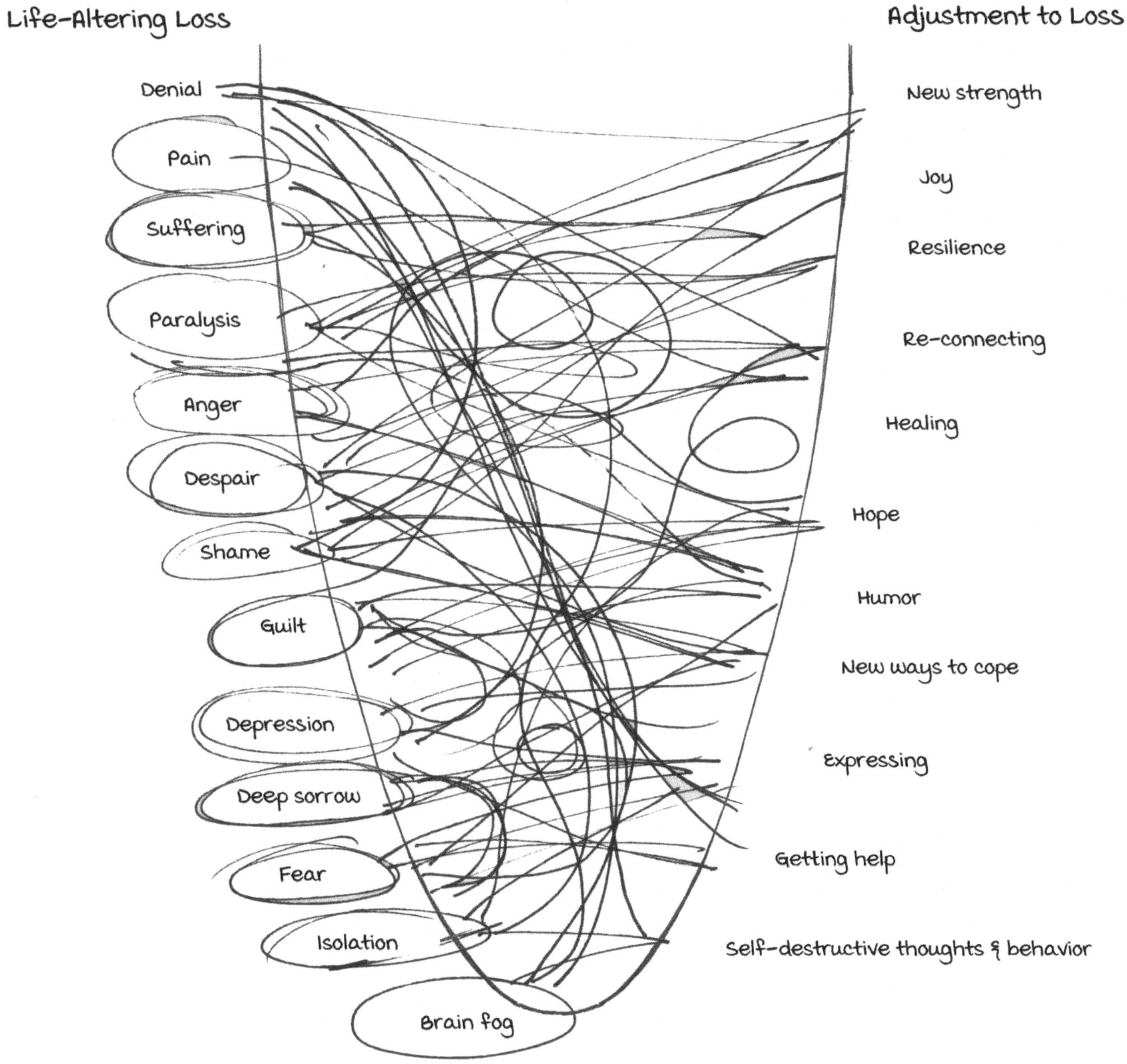

The truth about grief and grieving is that it is MESSY, difficult, and often lonely. These is *no* set timeline, pattern or process for grieving. Grief that comes from the traumatic losses connected to adoption and foster care is often harder at the time the loss occurred and includes a lot of secondary losses that continue to surface as you age and mature. This can create BIG or intense feelings that can be hard to express.

List the feelings you have connected to your loss and grief:

....

....

....

....

....

....

....

....

List all the strengths and ways you've worked hard to cope and survive from the traumatic losses and experiences you've been through:

....

....

....

....

....

....

....

....

List the friends and people you can share your deep feelings with:

....

....

....

....

....

....

....

....

Avoiding or repressing BIG emotions is like a volcano that never gets to let out any steam!

MY EI

You have experienced more loss or trauma than the average teen who has not been adopted or in foster care. Strengthening your 'emotional muscles' or 'emotional intelligence' will help you better understand yourself, your emotions and your relationships.

Consider the following statements and put 'never', 'sometimes' or 'always' in front of each one.

I find it easy to put my feelings into words. ....

My feelings are clear to me at any given moment. ....

I am emotionally balanced. ....

I accept responsibility for my actions and reactions. ....

Even when I'm upset, I'm aware of my feelings and actions. ....

When I'm angry at someone I can manage my hurtful impulses. ....

I care about what happens to others. ....

I consider the impact my feelings and actions have on others. ....

I can easily sense when I'm getting angry or upset. ....

I'm able to express love and show affection. ....

I'm generally a kind and friendly person. ....

I find it easy to share my deep feelings with people I trust. ....

I'm OK with others expressing strong emotions. ....

My moods and emotions impact those around me.. ....

I have empathy when others are hurt or upset. ....

I can recover quickly after a stressful event or conflict. ....

I'm getting emotionally stronger each and every day.
Building healthy relationships takes practice!

WHAT IS EMOTIONAL INTELLIGENCE?

The wonderful news about emotional intelligence is that it can be learned and strengthened at any point in our life. For teens who have experienced adoption, foster care or kinship, it's even more important to have the skills and tools to manage BIG feelings and emotions. You have experienced more loss, trauma and 'hard stuff' than many people experience in a whole lifetime. Understanding and healing from all that you have been through and experienced requires you know an awful lot about your own feelings and how to best manage and express those emotions. This may include unprocessed early trauma and neglect that is outside your conscious awareness.

The skills of emotional intelligence include our ability to:

- experience emotions—to identify and recognize the feelings and emotions of oneself and others
- have 'thoughts' about our feelings—to identify, name and communicate our feelings, and recognize the interplay between our internal feelings and our thought processes
- use our emotional wisdom—to use our emotional knowledge and experiences to build healthy relationships and meaningful social interactions
- manage our inner emotional world—to be open to feelings, and to modulate them; to modulate arousal levels and down-regulate after a stress response or up-arouse into a pleasure state.

my thoughts impact my feelings. my feelings impact my thoughts. Learning to understand this interconnection increase my Self-Awareness and strengthens my meaningful relationships

GRIEF AND MY FAMILY

We first learn about grief, loss and how to express our BIG feelings inside our family. What did you learn about expressing strong feelings, such as anger, fear, sadness, pain, grief and loneliness, during your childhood?

Growing up in my family, when something sad or bad happened, this is how my family responded or coped:

....

....

....

Growing up in my family, when I was sad or hurt or upset, I would:

....

....

....

Growing up in my family, this is how we responded to conflict and anger:

....

....

....

Growing up in my family, these are the messages I got about expressing feelings like sadness, hurt, anger or loneliness:

....

....

....

These are the things I would change about how BIG feelings like grief, sorrow, pain and sadness were expressed in my family:

....

....

....

my feelings are temporary. They come and go. Learning to express my feelings to people I care about takes practice.

MY GRIEF QUESTIONNAIRE

Describe your beliefs about grief and grieving. Where did you get these beliefs?

When you think about all the losses and trauma that you experienced from being adopted or in foster care, name all the feelings you have connected to those experiences.

It's common for the issues and feelings connected to adoption and foster care to intensify during your teen years. You're trying to figure out who you are and what kind of life you want. This requires the emotional and psychological 'work' of putting all the pieces of your life together. Easier said than done! What makes this task difficult for you?

What do you do with the sometimes BIG or intense feelings that can come with being adopted or in foster care?

What things have been most helpful for you when you've felt deep sorrow, grief, loneliness or despair?

It is helpful to NOT be alone when you're in deep pain and grief. Who are the people you trust and care about and who can support you when you're doing the emotional work of grieving or when you are in a lot of pain?

....

....

....

....

Unacknowledged or blocked grief can look like anger, chronic agitation and rage. What can you do to express these intense feelings so you can release them from your body, heart and mind?

....

....

....

....

Significant life losses occur at a particular season, time, date and place. Anniversary reactions are important reminders of our grief and loss. In what ways do you experience these anniversary triggers and how do you cope with the memories and feelings?

....

....

....

....

Birthdays and Mother's Day are often tricky for teens who have been adopted or are in foster care. What thoughts and feelings do these days trigger for you and what has helped you to cope or manage those feelings?

....

....

....

....

Developing a ritual to support and honor your grief process is helpful. Creating a poster, collage, writing a letter or poem about your loss, grief and feelings helps you identify and express what's inside.

Sorrow shared is halved, while joy shared is doubled!

SOMETIMES I WISH...

It's OK to think about, wonder and wish for things. Lots of teens who are in foster care or adopted 'wish' that things could have been different. You may wonder who your birth/first parents are, what they look like, where they are now or what it would have been like to be parented by them. Or you may wish to see a former foster parent or a sibling. Write down all your wonderings and wishes in YOUR wishing cloud.

It's hard not knowing or seeing the people I care about.
It's OK to think about and miss them!

THE LANGUAGE OF EMOTION

To effectively express deep feelings of pain, loss and grief, we need to learn and use the language of emotion. Use these feeling words to identify and express the emotions that you experience in your day to day life so you become more comfortable identifying and expressing emotions. Circle all the feelings that you have felt this month. Create a Feelings Journal or find trusted people who care about you to share some of the more intense and painful emotions.

HAPPY

- Excited
- Cheerful
- Energetic
- Playful
- Silly
- Grateful
- Loving
- Optimistic
- Creative

SAD

- Upset
- Heavy
- Tearful
- Sorrowful
- Lonely
- Bored
- Tired
- Guilty
- Depressed

STRONG

- Secure
- Confident
- Empowered
- Determined
- Powerful
- Unique
- Energetic
- Ambitious
- Adventurous

CALM

- Peaceful
- Secure
- Content
- Trusting
- Hopeful
- Valuable
- Relaxed
- Aware
- Thoughtful

ANGRY

- Frustrated
- Annoyed
- Mad
- Resentful
- Furious
- Bitter
- Critical
- Hateful
- Hostile

HURT

- Rejected
- Let down
- Abandoned
- Crushed
- Punished
- Abused
- Damaged
- Criticized
- Ashamed

ANXIOUS

- Worried
- Nervous
- Stressed
- Frozen
- Troubled
- Inadequate
- Embarrassed
- Desperate

SCARED

- Fearful
- Alone
- Overwhelmed
- Hurt
- Helpless
- Lost
- Victimized
- Insignificant
- Terrorized

The most complex organ in the universe is the human brain. Understanding and mastering your own mind takes time and practice!

MY HURT JAR

We can't heal if we can't identify our hurt and pain. We've got to 'name it' to 'tame it!' Hurt and pain are always part of grief and loss in adoption and foster care. Unacknowledged hurt and pain can make you feel bitter, angry and resentful. Fill your 'hurt jar' with all the things that have hurt you and find someone you trust and care about to share what's inside.

Holding on to old hurt and pain doesn't help me feel better—I deserve to be happy and have fun like everyone else!

IF MY FEELINGS COULD TALK

You are wired to feel. Your emotions are an important form of communication. Your feelings are always telling you something about what YOU need, what you want or what you're concerned about. When you're aware of what you're feeling, you can identify what you need and find ways to meet those needs in healthy ways. Complete the following sentences to learn what YOUR feelings are communicating to you.

LONELINESS might be telling me I need CONNECTION.

SHAME might be telling me I need SELF-COMPASSION.

ANXIETY might be telling me I need BRAVERY.

RESENTMENT might be telling me I need FORGIVENESS.

SADNESS might be telling me I need TO CRY.

EMPTINESS might be telling me I need LOVE and HOPE.

STRESS might be telling me I need ....

ANGER might be telling me I need ....

HURT might be telling me I need ....

GUILT might be telling me I need ....

my feelings give me important information about what I want and need in my life and relationships.

WHY AM I SO ANGRY?

Pain and hurt are always underneath anger! Unacknowledged loss, pain and trauma can easily turn into anger. Sometimes it turns into a LOT of anger! Teens who have been adopted or in foster care have suffered profound losses that need to be acknowledged, grieved and healed.

- Anger is a normal part of the grief and grieving process.
- Anger is an important emotion that gives our body energy.
- Learning to express anger in a healthy way is important.
- Expressing and releasing anger helps us to grow and heal.

Fill in your answers to the following questions:

If my ANGER could talk, this is what it would say!

I'm angry because ....

I'm angry because ....

I'm angry because ....

I'm angry because ....

I'm angry because ....

I'm angry because ....

If my ANGER could tell me what it needs, this is what it would say!

I need ....

I need ....

I need ....

I need ....

I need ....

Learning how to express my deep hurt and anger the right way is an important part of my healing process!

WHAT TO DO WITH ALL THIS GRIEF AND ANGER

Your body has experienced a lot of toxic stress, hurt and trauma. It's important for the body, heart and mind to learn to release and discharge pain and suffering. Practice doing one of the following each day!

- Pound a drum, pound a pillow, punch a punching bag.
- Listen to sad songs or watch a sad movie and let yourself cry.
- Exercise, run, ride, bike, kayak, hike; get your heart rate up and allow your body to circulate toxic stress out of your sensory system.
- Draw, paint or color a picture of your pain, hurt or anger.
- Make an Anger Jar and fill it with all the things that have hurt you.
- Bang on pots and pans and yell.
- Write in a journal allowing yourself to vent and express everything.
- Throw wet sponges at your garage door and with each throw identify something or someone that has hurt you or caused you pain.
- Write a poem or song or story about your pain, loss, grief or trauma.
- Get a professional massage to release stress and toxins.
- Breathe deeply and slowly for five minutes, helping the body find calm and balance.
- Create a 'Feelings Space' in your room where ALL feelings are OK and all feelings get to be expressed, validated and released.
- Create a collage or vision board that includes your 'trauma to triumph' story and include a positive vision for yourself and your future.
- Do a guided meditation that takes your body and mind on a calm and healing journey.

It feels good to let my body, heart and mind release old pain and hurt!

— Chapter 5 —

IDENTITY

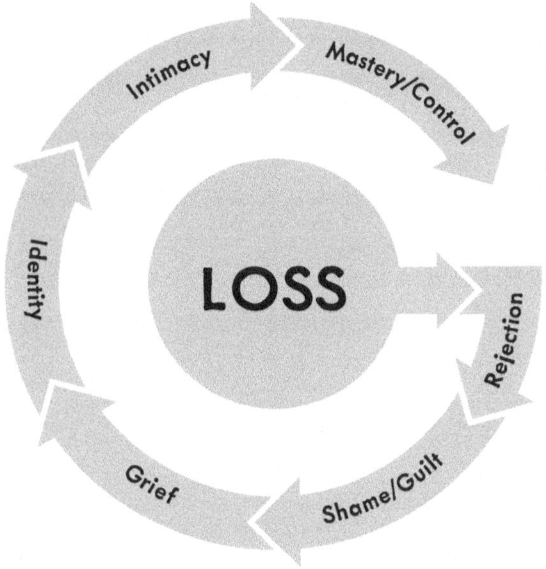

The fourth spoke in the Seven Core Issues wheel is identity. Self-identity is at the heart of the human journey. We are all on this quest to understand who we are, where we fit and how to be the hero in our own life story.

Teens who are adopted or in foster/kinship care:

- lack information about their history, which makes figuring out their identity more challenging, frustrating and complex
- lack connection to birth/first parents and extended family, creating a disconnection from important parts of their lineage and heritage, including medical, genetic, cultural, ethnic/racial and historical information and relationships
- have missing information that can create distress, anxiety, suffering and confusion regarding who they feel they are, or identity formation
- may 'try on' various identities in search of belonging, connection and 'self-identity'
- in their search for identity may try to connect with parts of their past and history. Trying

to more deeply understand 'what happened' and 'why it happened' is an attempt to understand their complete story.

Know this:

- Your identity belongs to YOU.
- YOU are the narrator of your story. The pen is in your hand!
- Use YOUR words, thoughts, feelings and strengths to tell your story.

MY IDENTITY QUESTIONNAIRE

Describe yourself in a few short sentences:

....

....

....

How do you think those who know you well would describe you?

....

....

....

Identity includes: your values, beliefs, self-image, gender identification and role, social identity, racial/ethnic/cultural heritage, physical characteristics and body image, sexuality and sexual orientation, personality traits and strengths/talents. In other words, identity is complex and unique to each person. Today, using the above puzzle pieces, how would you describe your identity?

....

....

....

....

....

How would you have described yourself as a child?

....

....

....

How has being adopted or in foster care impacted your identity?

....

....

....

What parts of your identity are connected to your parents and family?

....

....

....

What parts of your identity are connected to your birth/first parents and those familial trees?

....

....

....

As a teen, you have a lot of questions, thoughts and feelings about your identity and your future. Understanding your past helps you better understand all the parts of who you are and helps you build the best future for yourself. What parts of your identity still feel like a mystery to you?

....

....

....

What would you change about your identity?

....

....

....

Who or what has helped you form your identity? Who were your role models? And why?

....

....

....

If your parents are from a different race/ethnic background, how has being raised by them impacted your identity?

....

....

....

I AM ME! I am enough! I am good! I am resilient! I am loveable! I am strong!

WORDS HAVE POWER

Words have power! They can build us up and help us feel strong, smart and important. Or they can tear us down and make us feel small, stupid and worthless. In the left column below, write down all the negative words you have used in the past to describe yourself. Then in the right column, write down all the strengths and positive characteristics and qualities that you have. Use this list each day to be more positive within yourself and to remind yourself of the power of YOUR words.

Negative

Positive

FOCUSED ON MY MISTAKES	FOCUSED ON MY STRENGTHS

Change your thoughts and you'll change your world!

PIECES OF ME

Building an identity is like putting together a big, complicated puzzle. There are a great many different kinds of pieces so it takes a long time. Teens who are adopted or in foster care may be missing pieces of their puzzle. This makes the emotional work of identity development more complex. Some teens may feel that their identity is unfinished or incomplete.

Write down all the pieces of your identity in the figure below.

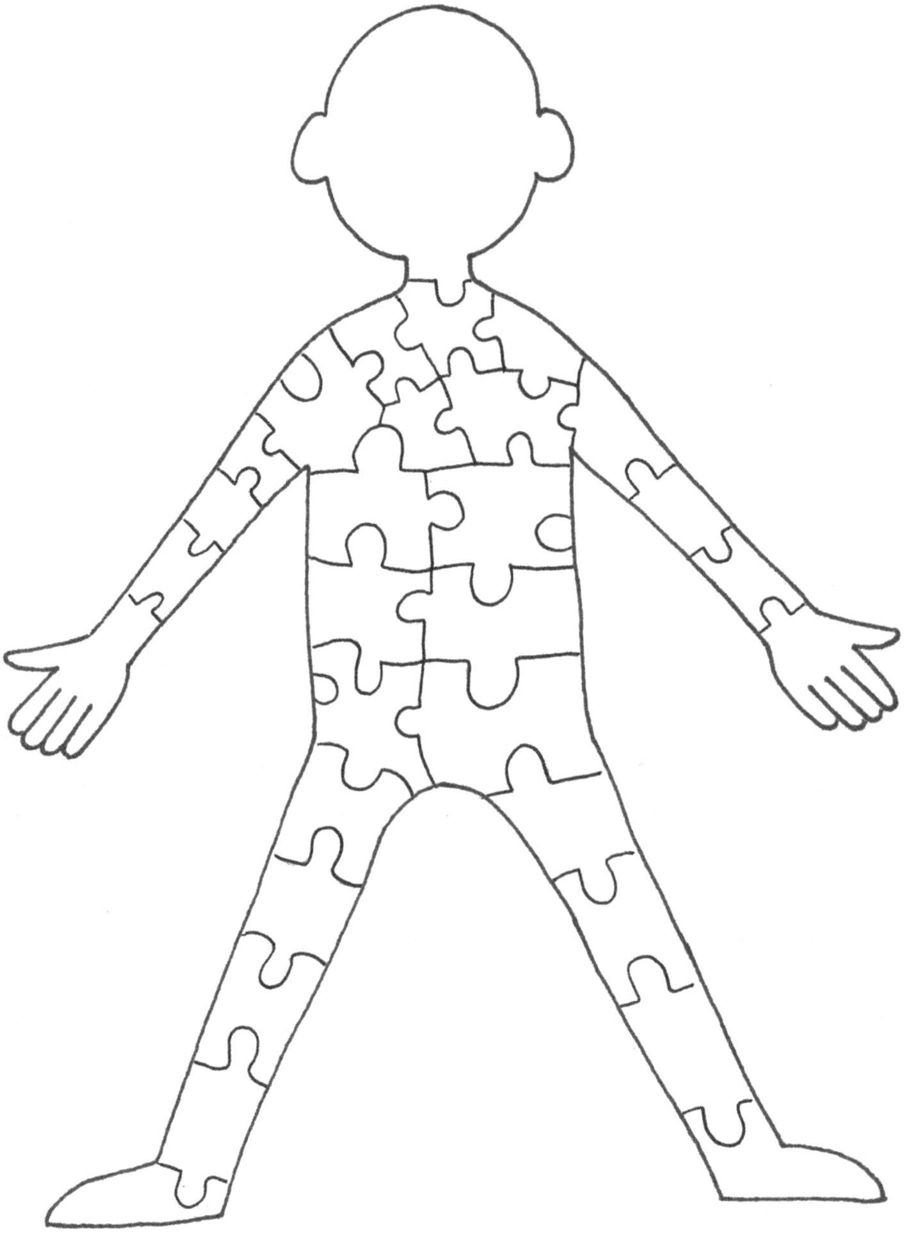

my identity belongs to me. It's my job to figure out who I Am and What I want to do with my life!

WHAT'S IN A NAME?

Our name is an important part of our identity. It's the symbol for who we are and it's how others identify us. It's also a way to identify where we belong. Parents and families name their children as a way to claim them into the family. If you were adopted, your name may have been changed by your parents. If you are in foster care, you may be disconnected from your birth/first parents and may not know much right now about where your name comes from.

What is your full name?

....

Who gave you your name?

....

Is there special meaning behind your name or were you named after someone?

....

How do you feel about your name?

....

Did you have another name or what was the name your birth/first parents gave you?

....

Do you know why your birth/first parents gave you that name?

....

If your name was changed, how do you feel about your name being changed?

....

Do you have a copy of your original birth certificate? What is the name you were given at birth?

....

Do you have a nickname and where did you get that nickname?

....

How do you feel about the various names you've been given and/or chosen?

....

I AM the one building and creating my identity. my identity belongs to me!

SOCIAL IDENTITY VS SELF-IDENTITY

Social identity: How I'm viewed by others or the outside world.

Self-identity: How I view myself.

Teens who are adopted or in foster care have been bombarded with lots of mixed messages, everything from 'You're so lucky, I wish I was adopted' to 'How terrible, I feel so sorry for you' to 'Don't you wanna go find your real parents?'

These confusing and often negative messages from the outside world can make you feel bad, not 'real', damaged, deserving of pity, needing to be grateful or negative about yourself. These labels from society may become part of your self-identity.

Let's explore and unpack the negative messages you may have internalized from the outside world. Remember, YOU are the expert in your own life and story.

How do others view you because you're adopted or in foster or kinship care?

....

....

....

What are some of the messages or comments that others have made about you being adopted or in foster or kinship care?

....

....

....

Do you think others would view you differently if you were born into your family?

....

....

....

What are some of the messages or comments you hear from TV, movies or social media about teens who are adopted or in foster or kinship care?

....

....

....

How do you decide when to tell others about your adoption or foster care story?

....

....

....

How do you think people's view of you would change if you tell them?

....

....

....

Who else knows about your adoption or foster care story and would they treat you differently if they didn't know?

....

....

....

As a teen, do you have the right to search for missing pieces of your past or identity?

....

....

....

When do you tell someone you're dating that you were adopted or in foster care and will it matter?

....

....

....

Here are three things you can do:

- Remember your story and every part of your history belongs to you. You decide what to tell, when to tell and how to tell the different parts of YOUR story.
- If you're feeling uncomfortable or anxious about sharing your story or history, listen to your body and feelings and be protective of yourself.
- Remember that you are not here to please other people and that you don't have to answer everyone's questions. They don't know how it feels to be YOU!

my identity does not belong to other people. I get to decide which parts of me I share with others!

MY SOCIAL IDENTITY

Your social identity is how YOU 'think' you are viewed by others. Sometimes teens who are adopted or in foster care can spend a lot of time focusing on what other people think about them. It can be exhausting trying to build an identity around what other people think or want. Write down all the words, labels and feelings in each of the circles based on how you 'think' people in those categories view you.

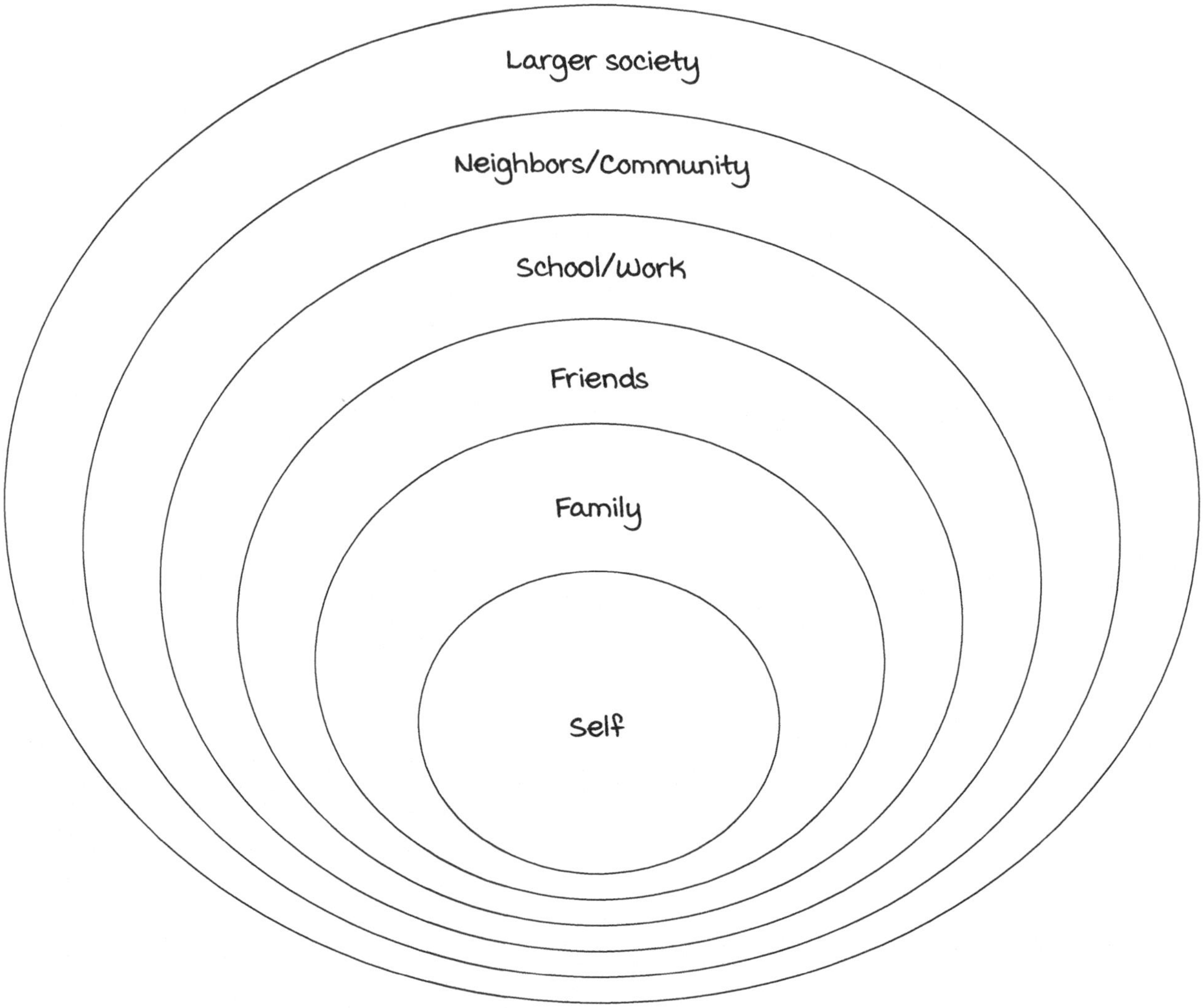

I cannot control how outsiders see me. I focus my energy on becoming the me I want to become!

MY SELF-IDENTITY

Your self-identity is how you view yourself. How YOU view yourself is what's most important since your identity belongs to YOU! After exploring your 'social identity', let's try and get rid of any of the negative messages that you may have internalized from others. Remember, they're not the experts on YOU and they're not in charge of building your identity! Write down all the strengths, characteristics, words and feelings that you would use to define yourself in each of the circles.

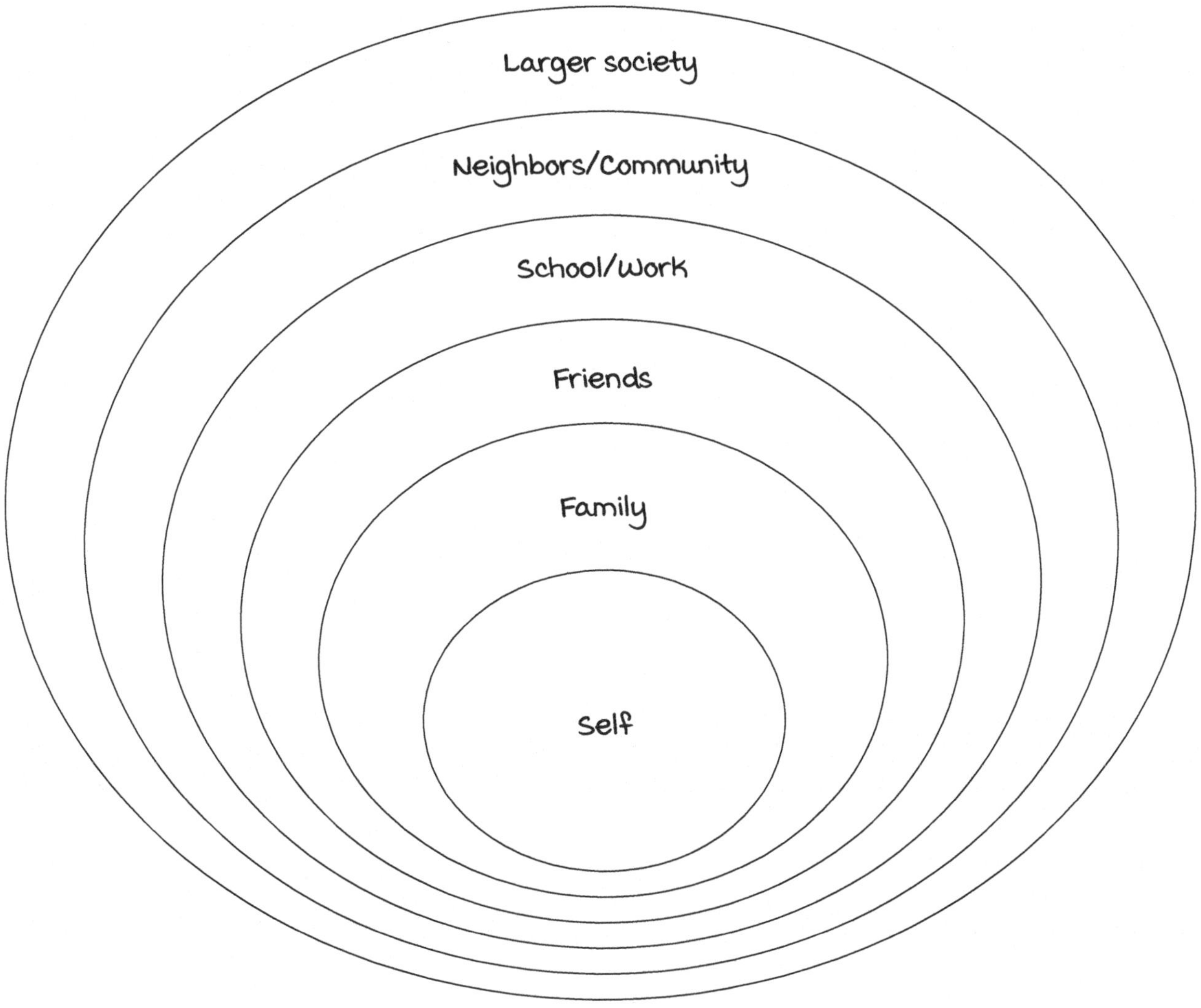

Great news! I have lots of time to work on my identity. I get to 'try on' different ways of being to see what feels the best and most authentic to me!

ONE AMAZING ME!

You got 50% of your DNA from your birth/first mother and 50% of your DNA from your birth/first father. You are a unique blend of their DNA, which carries DNA from their ancestors. We all get certain things from our genetics like our body type, appearance and certain personality traits. We also get a lot of our identity, values and beliefs from the family that raises us. You are a unique blend of all the trees that helped to make ONE AMAZING YOU!

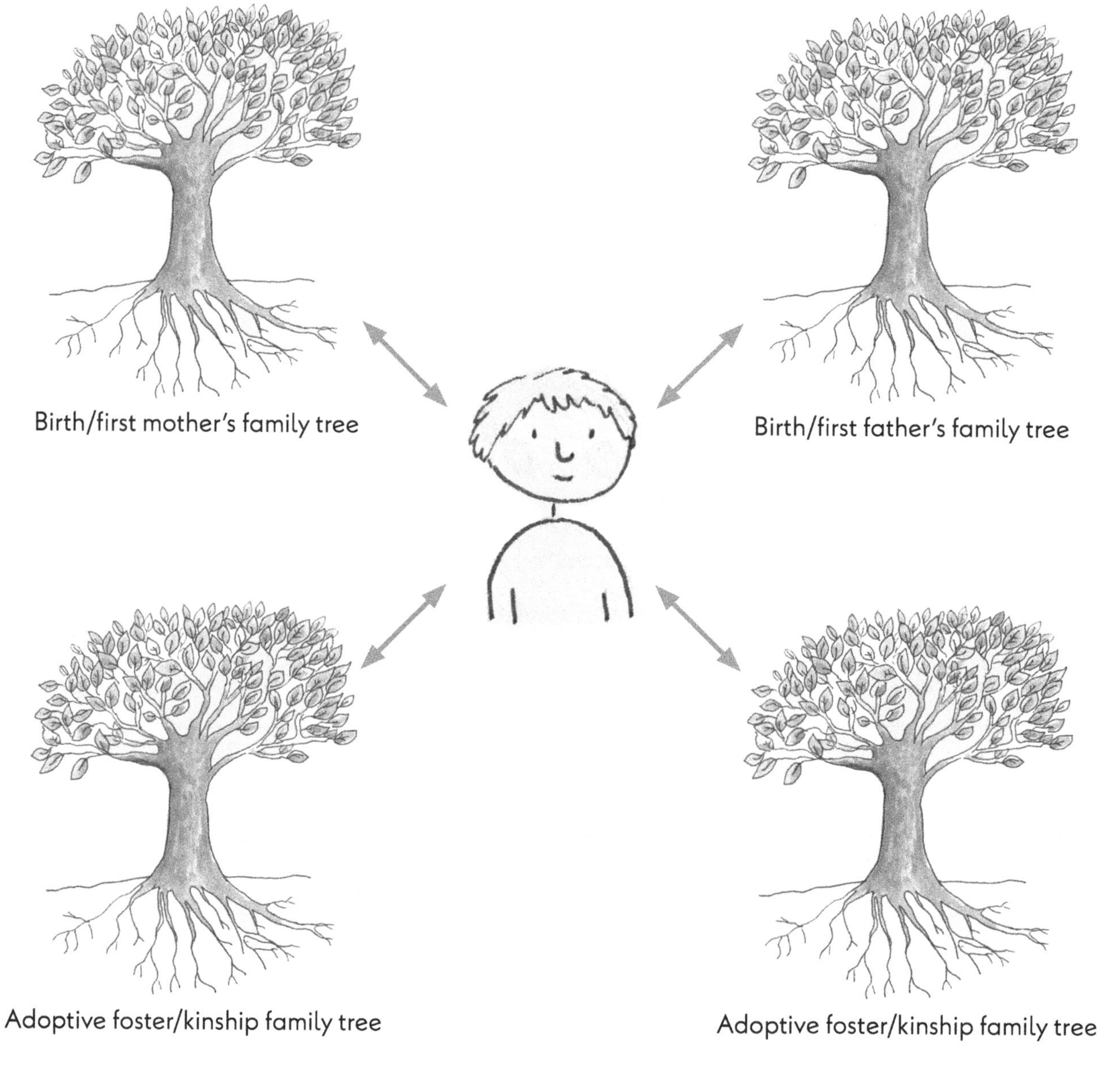

What are some of the things you think you got from your birth/first mother?

....

....

....

....

What are some of the things you think you got from your birth/first father?

....

....

....

....

What are some of the things you think you get from your mom?

....

....

....

....

What are some of the things you think you get from your dad?

....

....

....

....

I AM a unique being in this world and I'm a beautiful blend of all the people and families who have loved and supported me!

RACE, IDENTITY AND TRANSRACIAL ADOPTIONS

The majority of transracial adoptions are white families adopting children of color (Latin, Asian or African heritage). This can sometimes make things harder for adoptees because it's easier for outsiders to 'see' that you were adopted. You may get more looks, stares, questions and comments. What we've learned from transracial adoptees who have shared their experiences is that there are quite a few things that can make building a positive racial/ethnic identity more challenging.

- 'Being a child/teen of color in a predominately white family, in a white neighborhood, in a white school, was really difficult at times!'
- 'Everyone expected me to be grateful.'
- 'I felt different.'
- 'My parents didn't talk about race; they minimized the racial differences.'
- 'I didn't feel comfortable in my own skin; I wanted to be white.'
- 'When I got teased or bullied because of my appearance or race, I didn't know what to do or how to defend myself.'
- 'I didn't know who I looked like; I didn't have any family that looked like me.'
- 'It was hard to feel good about how I looked when everything around me was so white.'

What have been the benefits about being a transracial adoptee?

....

....

....

....

What have been the challenges about being a transracial adoptee?

....

....

....

....

What are your thoughts, beliefs and feelings about your ethnic and racial heritage?

....

....

....

....

What kinds of things have your parents done to help you understand and connect to your ethnic and racial heritage and history? What additional things would you like them to do?

What role models, mentors and connections do you have to your ethnic and racial heritage? How have they impacted your identity?

What kinds of things have you done to help strengthen your connection to your racial, ethnic and cultural community?

What foods, books, magazines, movies, music and art have helped you learn and connect to your racial, ethnic or cultural heritage?

How would you describe your racial or ethnic identity? How do you feel about that aspect of your identity?

How have other people's views or opinions impacted your identity?

....

....

....

....

How often do you talk about race, racism and white conditioning or privilege? What are the themes in these conversations? How have your thoughts and feelings changed since becoming a teen?

....

....

....

....

How do you think you would be different if you were raised inside your birth/first family or a family that was the same ethnicity or race as you?

....

....

....

....

How do your family and extended family talk about white privilege, racism and adoption?

....

....

....

....

When your friends or peers talk about race, ethnicity and adoption, what words, stereotypes, jokes or beliefs are shared? How do you respond?

....

....

....

....

Tips for teens and parents

- Educate yourself and your family about racism and prejudice.
  - What will you do when someone calls you a racial slur or tells you to go back where you came from?
  - As a parent, you need to help ensure your child feels safe and secure both physically and emotionally in their home, school and neighborhood.
- Talk openly and honestly about differences, diversity and racism.
  - Acknowledge and celebrate differences.
  - Think about where you live, where you go to church, where your teen goes to school, what your doctor/dentist/coaches/teachers/youth leaders look like. Your teen needs to see lots of positive reflections and mirror images of themselves.
- Celebrate race/ethnicity/culture through:
  - books, TV shows, pictures, historical figures, stories, rituals, foods, music and holidays that celebrate and honor your teen's heritage
  - role models and relationships with mentors who have 'lived experience' connected to your teen's race/ethnicity/culture. They can mentor and coach your teen with coping strategies and help them develop a positive racial/ethnic identity.
- Prepare for racism and prejudice.
  - Teens who have not been prepared for racism and bullying often feel demeaned, scared and/or ashamed about the color of their skin, or the shape of their eyes or the differences in their appearance from the white culture. They may not know what to do, what to say or how to act when racism occurs.
  - Find a group, mentor or coach who can assist you and your teen in developing the knowledge, attitudes and skills necessary to defend against racism and prejudice. Both you and your teen can learn to become advocates to create a more inclusive, diverse and anti-racist community and culture.

My racial/ethnic identity belongs to me! It's important for me to feel good about how I look and where I came from. Understanding all the different parts of me helps me feel positive and strong!

ADOPTEE FAMILY WHEEL

You are a wonderful blend of all the parents who helped to make YOU! Write down the names, birth dates, country and race/ethnic heritage for everyone on your adoptee Family Wheel.

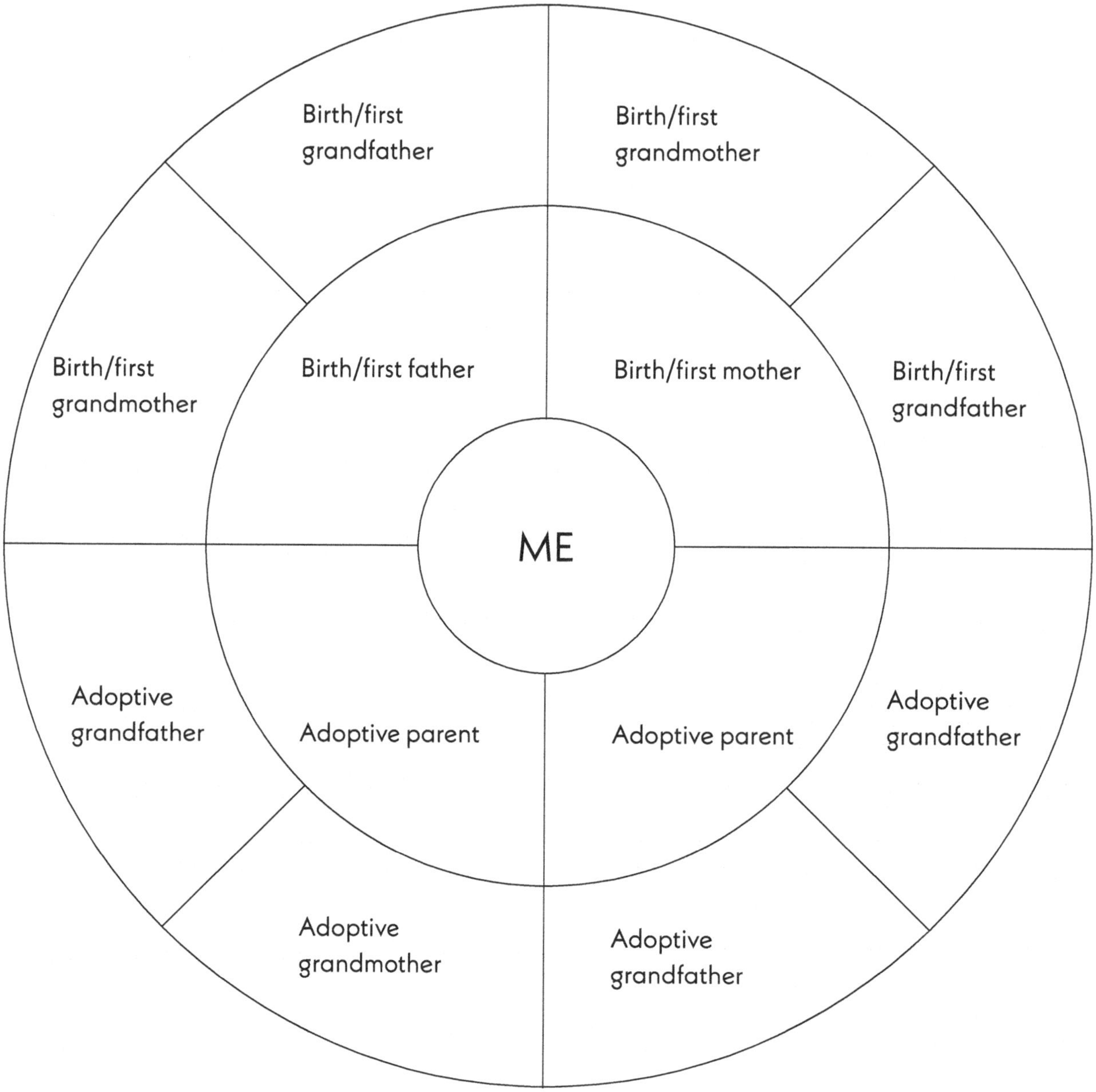

my life story is...complicated! missing pieces of my story can trigger feelings of loss, confusion, sadness or anger. I have a right to the truth of my story.

TO SEARCH OR NOT TO SEARCH!

The emotional work of building an identity requires that we 'search for self'. We must do the internal work of exploring all the different parts of our story and inner world. Secrets, misinformation and disconnection from our roots and history can lead to identity confusion, shame and distress. Many teens begin to search for missing facts, people, information and puzzle pieces from their past. Since every teen is unique in how they think and feel about their own adoption or foster care experience, there is no right or wrong answer to the question, 'Should I search or not search?'

Some teens are searching for who they look like or their ethnic/racial heritage. Some are searching for lost siblings. Some teens are searching as a way to remember their old house, friends, neighborhood or pets. Some teens are searching for their birth/first mother or father because they want more details about what happened and why it happened. Some teens are searching for lost connections to a former foster parent, coach, adoption agency or mentor.

Searching for the missing pieces to one's story and history is a search for identity, rootedness and wholeness. Only you can know what YOU are searching for and what things from your past are important to you.

Teens who are adopted or in foster care often have a lot of questions about what happened and why it happened and how decisions were made that impacted their life. What are some of the questions that you have?

....

....

....

....

How do you think you would feel if you had answers to all the questions you have about your adoption or foster care story or about your birth/first parents?

....

....

....

....

Have you been able to talk openly to your parents about all the questions and feelings you have about searching or not searching? How have they responded?

....

....

....

....

Remember, it's OK to search and it's OK not to search. What are some of your fears or concerns about searching?

....

....

....

....

What are some of the benefits of searching?

....

....

....

....

Searching for answers to questions about your past can trigger feelings of confusion, anxiety, hurt or anger. What are three things you can do to cope with the emotional rollercoaster of searching for the missing pieces of your story?

....

....

....

....

Who is supporting your emotional work of building an identity? Who can you vent to or share your feelings, concerns and challenges with? How have they been helpful?

....

....

....

....

Ways to take good care of YOURSELF:

- Start an Identity Journal: fill it without judgment.
- Find caring and trusting people who can support your journey.
- Build protective boundaries around confused or unhealed parts of yourself.
- Find mentors or friends with similar stories who can support you.
- Find a support group or therapist who understands early trauma, loss and adoption or foster care.

I get to decide when I want to search and when I want to 'not search'!

— Chapter 6 —

INTIMACY

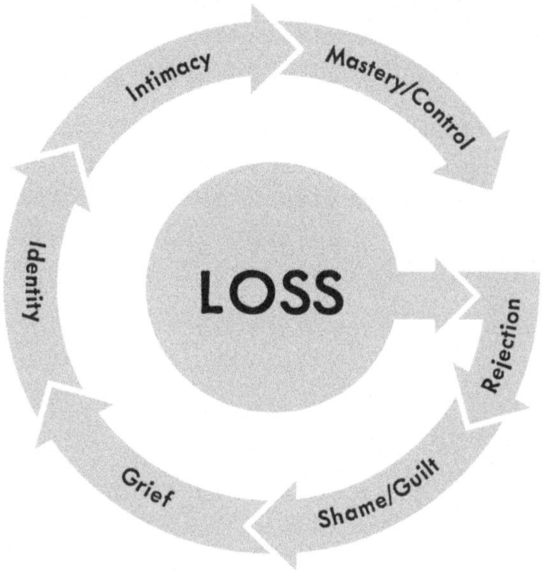

The fifth spoke in the Seven Core Issues wheel is intimacy. One of our strongest needs is our need to feel deeply connected to people who love and care about us. Learning the skills to create trusting, loving and caring relationships takes practice.

Teens who are adopted or in foster/kinship care:

- find that getting close and trusting people can be hard when they've been hurt, abused, abandoned or rejected in the past
- have missing pieces to their identity that can make it hard to get close to others
- need to develop a strong social network of peers; being adopted or in foster care can make them feel different from their peers
- can easily fear more rejection and abandonment, especially if they have experienced attachment disruptions and multiple moves in foster care. They may decide that getting emotionally close to others is too risky or scary

- find it hard to know when to share and may question whether they are loveable or deserve to be loved; being vulnerable may include sharing difficult parts of their past and story
- often feel that rejecting others first is a way to keep themselves safe, but it can also limit the depth of their connections or relationships.

Know this:

- YOU both need and deserve to be loved and cared about.
- Learning how to create deep meaningful connections takes practice.
- Becoming more knowledgeable and comfortable with your past, your feelings and your identity will help YOU build strong, loving connections.

MY INTIMACY QUESTIONNAIRE

How do you define emotional closeness or intimacy?

What qualities do you need from someone to build a trusting and caring relationship?

What qualities do you bring to a trusting and caring relationship?

What do you think a healthy and caring relationship looks like?

What qualities and characteristics in your close friendships are important to you?

How has being adopted or in foster care impacted your close relationships?

Who are your role models for healthy intimate relationships? And why?

How do you handle conflict or disagreements in your close relationships?

....

....

....

What fears or concerns do you have about getting close to others?

....

....

....

What obstacles, defenses or barriers do you use to avoid closeness or intimacy?

....

....

....

How do you accept or address your own or another person's flaws or differences?

....

....

....

How do you know if your close relationships are healthy or toxic?

....

....

....

As you learn more about yourself and your identity, how do you think your close relationships will change?

....

....

....

Learning to feel good about myself is an important part of the healing process.

MY LOVE JAR

What are YOUR values? Values help to guide our behaviors and actions so we can live a happy and healthy life. Some examples of values are honesty, responsibility, respect, empathy, dependability, curiosity, generosity, friendliness, resilience. The easiest way to figure out YOUR values is to begin by identifying all the things you love. List all the things you love in the jar below.

my love jar is filled with all the things I love. As I continue to be brave and try new things, I will discover lots more things to add to my Love Jar!

THE DIFFERENT KINDS OF INTIMACY

There are different kinds of intimacy. You have a different level of intimacy with your parents vs strangers; or with a close friend vs a neighbor; or with your girl/boyfriend vs your teacher. As you grow and learn new emotional skills, your relationships will strengthen and deepen.

Different kinds of intimacy:

- Social intimacy
  - Our friends and peers help us to feel a sense of belonging and connection. Building and maintaining these supportive relationships requires social and emotional skills.
- Emotional intimacy
  - Deep feelings of closeness where we can be authentically ourselves. Sharing our intimate thoughts, feelings, vulnerabilities, beliefs and goals.
- Intellectual intimacy
  - Exchanging thoughts and ideas about things we really care about, such as social issues, movies, songs, books, poems, art.
- Physical intimacy
  - Being physically affectionate using touch, hugging, cuddling or holding hands.
- Sexual intimacy
  - Teens may confuse intimacy with the act of sex. Sex can occur with or without emotional intimacy. Sex without emotional intimacy might include rape, a one-night stand or sex without love, trust or warmth.
- Spiritual intimacy
  - Sharing the same religious or spiritual belief systems. Feeling unity and mutual commitment to those values and teachings.

Intimacy means different things to different people. What kinds of experiences help you feel close or connected to others?

What do you need from someone in order to feel loved and cared about?

Are you comfortable communicating your needs and feelings to people who care about you? If no, why not?

....

....

....

What kinds of intimacy have been the most challenging for you?

....

....

....

What are three things you can do to strengthen your close relationships?

....

....

....

Knowing and understanding yourself helps you to know what you need in order to feel safe and loved by others. What are three things you want people close to you to understand about what you need from them?

....

....

....

Making mistakes in relationships is how we learn, change and grow!

Keep practicing!

INTIMACY AND MY MIND, HEART AND BODY

Each of us brings our own mind, heart and body into our close relationships. Our internal self-awareness allows us to communicate our wants and needs to those we love and trust. At the same time, we're also learning how to understand the wants and needs of others, and the emotional 'give and take' of those close relationships.

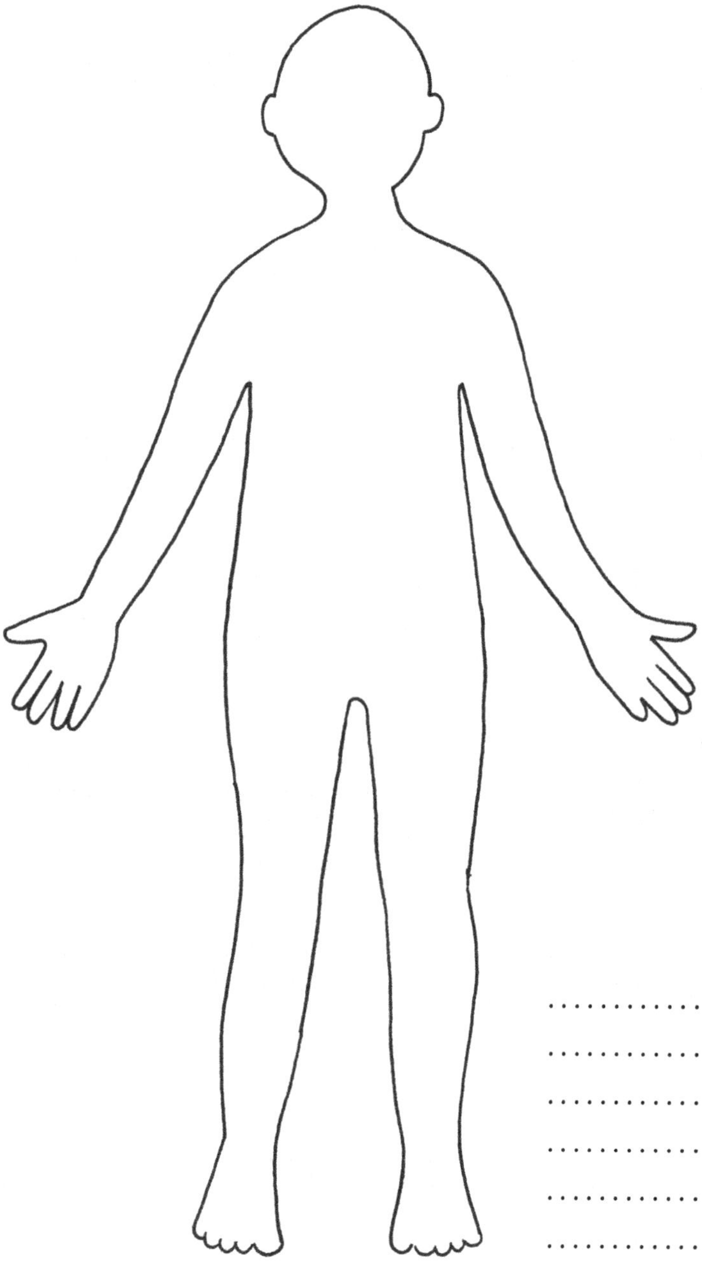

Mind
What thoughts, perceptions and belief systems do I have about myself or 'others' that either allow or dismiss emotional closeness or intimacy?

Heart
What needs and wants does my heart desire? Do I know what my heart needs from another? Do I communicate those needs and expectations?

Body
Is my body comfortable with emotional closeness and physical affection? Am I comfortable with safe, loving touch and affection?

....
....
....
....
....
....

You're built to feel, connect and love!

WHAT'S A HEALTHY RELATIONSHIP?

You have experienced more loss or trauma than the average teen who hasn't been adopted or fostered. It's important to create relationships that are healthy and make you feel loved and cared about. Your teen years are an important time to learn and practice healthy relationship skills.

Consider the following statements and put 'never', 'sometimes' or 'always' next to each one.

We treat each other as equals...

I feel liked and cared about by this person. ....

I feel physically safe with this person. ....

I feel emotionally safe with this person. ....

I can express my feelings openly and honestly. ....

When there's a conflict, we can share our feelings respectfully. ....

I can say 'no' when I'm not comfortable with something. ....

We have fun when we're together. ....

I can set healthy boundaries if I'm not comfortable with something. ....

I can share my vulnerable side without being judged. ....

I can be my 'real' self with this person.. ....

My needs and feelings are respected. ....

We communicate our hurt, upset or angry feelings in a respectful way where we both have an opportunity to express, learn and grow. ....

I deserve to feel safe, loved and respected in my relationships.

HOW WELL DO YOU KNOW ME?

Sometimes parents 'think' they know their teen better than they actually do. Find out how well your parents or caregivers really know YOU! Try asking them these questions.

1. What am I putting most of my energy into right now?
2. What personal issues am I trying to resolve?
3. What daily hassles irritate me?
4. Who has the most daily influence on my thoughts and behaviors?
5. Name my three closest friends.
6. Who would I confide in first if there were a serious problem?
7. What do I consider to be my greatest strengths?
8. What do I consider to be my greatest challenges or weaknesses?
9. What is my favorite time of day?
10. What are my top three favorite movies?
11. What is my favorite childhood story?
12. What is my favorite hobby or pastime?
13. What is my favorite color?
14. What is my favorite food or meal?
15. Who are my heroes? Why?
16. What is my favorite song, band or singer?
17. What are my three favorite books? Why?
18. What is my favorite television show?
19. How do I feel about my body and appearance?
20. Who was my first crush? First kiss?
21. What are my greatest fears or insecurities?
22. How do I feel about myself? And why do I feel this way?
23. What are some of my goals and dreams?
24. What is my most embarrassing moment?
25. How did I learn about the birds and the bees?
26. Who do I talk to about dating, break-ups, consent and safe sex?
27. What is my favorite holiday and why?
28. What do I most need to hear or feel from you (my parents or caregivers)?
29. How do I feel about being adopted or in foster/kinship care?
30. How often do I think about my birth/first parents?
31. What's been the hardest part about being adopted or in foster/kinship care?
32. Have I ever been bullied? What happened?
33. Are there things from my past that still cause hurt and pain today?
34. How do I feel about having been adopted or fostered by you?
35. If my life was a book, what would the title be?

If they could answer most of these questions, well done to them! They know you. The more questions that stumped them, the bigger the gap between them and you. Talking about deep feelings, values, complex issues and struggles takes practice. When parents become deep listeners, they will better know and understand their teen.

Be Curious! Be Silly! Be Bold! Be Creative! Be YOU!

THE REAL ME

Understanding who you are 'beneath the surface' helps you feel more secure and confident in your relationships. Human beings are built like an iceberg—we have a lot going on 'beneath the surface'. Humans have a prolonged adolescence to give teens lots of time to figure out who they are on the inside so they can build the kind of life and relationships that feel best to them. Fill in the iceberg below to help you discover the Real YOU!

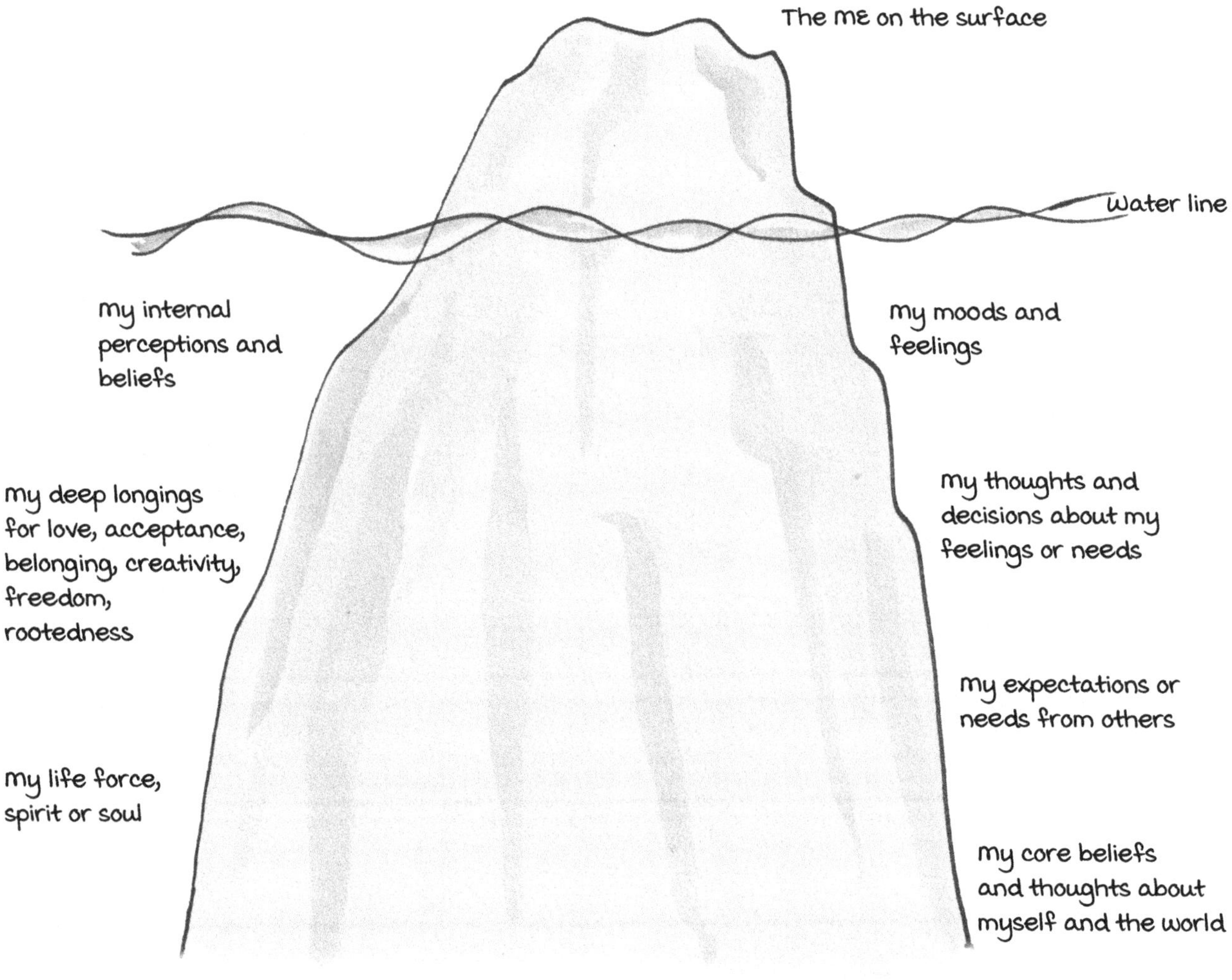

I am all the different parts of me! I get to explore and choose the me I am becoming!

TOOLS FOR HEALTHY COMMUNICATION

The most complex organ in the universe is the human mind. When two 'human minds' come together to communicate their values, needs, emotions and thoughts, things can sometimes get a bit messy. Post these guidelines for improving communication on your fridge or by your bed and practice, practice, practice!

- Be aware of YOUR mood and feelings. Make a 'date' to talk about a problem or conflict.
- Be aware of the other person's mood and feelings.
- Be responsible for your own feelings. Communicate them honestly, openly and effectively.
- Listen deeply to what the other person is sharing. Notice all the non-verbal messages.
- Listen to understand rather than listen to 'be right'.
- Be empathic. Let the person know you care about them and that it's OK to disagree sometimes.
- Identify communication barriers. Brainstorm solutions, take a break, reverse roles and try again later.
- Encourage differences and uniqueness.

Having healthy communication skills strengthens and deepens relationships.

MY TALKING HEART

Teens who have experienced early loss and trauma may hold a lot of painful, confusing and sometimes overwhelming thoughts and feelings inside their heart. It's common because those things are hard to talk about. Teaching your heart to talk about those hard or painful experiences is the best way to release old trauma or hurt. Start slowly, pick one thing in your heart, find a trusted and caring person and let your 'talking heart' share what it's been holding inside.

Feelings in my heart change over time. I check in with my heart every day so I know what my heart needs to feel safe, connected and loved.

— Chapter 7 —

MASTERY AND CONTROL

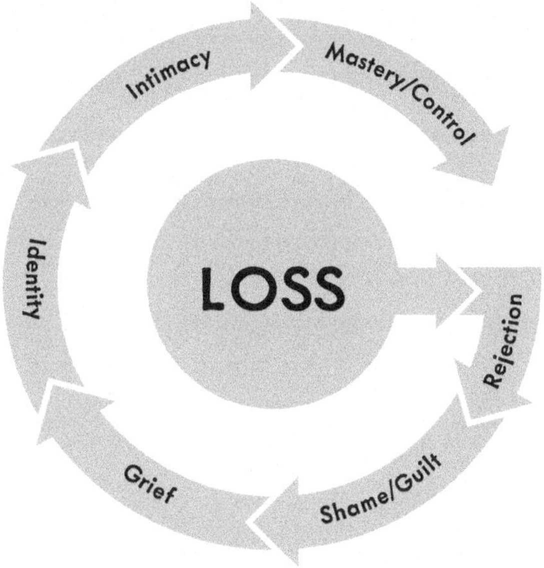

The last spoke in the Seven Core Issues wheel is mastery and control. We all have a need to feel powerful, strong and in control of who we are and our life path. The life-altering loss of one's birth/first parents and all the unnamed, unidentified and ungrieved losses can create feelings of powerlessness and a loss of control.

Teens who are adopted or in foster/kinship care:

- experience loss of control and power, leading to feelings of helplessness, anger, fear, shame, blame and powerlessness
- find that early losses and trauma that occur pre-verbally (as babies and toddlers) can create ongoing issues with power and control. Children need to feel a strong sense of mastery as they develop, learn and grow
- need to build their identity; missing pieces and parts of their history and story can create feelings of powerlessness and loss of control
- often 'fight' for more control as they're claiming their independence. If they arrived into

their family as an older child, they may have needs that went unmet. They may need more time to heal and grow in the family
- need to explore their strengths and needs to gain some control and power in their life, and work to communicate those needs to people they love and trust
- must understand that most people in the outside world have no idea what it 'really' feels like to be adopted or fostered. They may say hurtful or insensitive things.

Know this:

- Mastery includes claiming your own story and identity. YOU are the expert!
- Mastery is more like a marathon than a sprint! Go easy on yourself!

MY MASTERY AND CONTROL QUESTIONNAIRE

Words connected to mastery include empowered, resilient, powerful, knowledgeable, skillful and fulfilled. Describe specific areas in your life where you have experienced a sense of mastery.

....

....

....

....

What feelings and emotions are connected to your areas of mastery?

....

....

....

....

Words connected to control include self-doubt, anxiety, disempowered, insecure, vulnerable and unsafe. Describe past events when you experienced a loss of control.

....

....

....

....

What feelings and emotions did you experience during those times? What did you do with those emotions?

....

....

....

....

We all have a desire to have control and power in how our life unfolds. Describe some of the things that have happened in your life that have taken some of your control and power away.

....

....

....

....

Each of us has a unique response to the loss of power and control. What actions and behaviors are typical for you when you lose control and power over important things in your life?

One of the first steps towards mastery is knowing what brings you meaning and fulfillment. Describe three things that are most important in your life and how you've worked to achieve those things.

What barriers or obstacles did you experience along the way? How did you respond to those obstacles and barriers?

In what ways did you get your needs for control met in childhood and how did your parents or caregivers respond to sharing control with you?

Teens with a strong need for control may have had experiences where they had little or no control. They may have experienced trauma, violence, poor attachment, isolation, threats, bullying and powerlessness. These experiences can leave you avoiding closeness and using controlling behaviors to keep others away from your 'real' self. Describe how you have managed these emotional triggers in your close relationships.

In what ways has adoption, foster care or kinship created issues around mastery and control for you? How have you coped with these additional feelings or challenges?

....

....

....

....

All of the BIG and little losses connected to being adopted or in foster care can create feelings of powerlessness and a loss of control. Having parents, judges, social workers, therapists and others making life-altering decisions about you and your life can feel disempowering. Describe how you have tried to use your strengths and resilience to gain a sense of control and power in your life.

....

....

....

....

Gaining a sense of mastery is all about knowing, learning and understanding your SELF: your story, your beliefs, your identity, your values and your hopes and dreams. Mastery is not a destination, it's a process. YOU are already in the process of self-discovery. Write a positive mantra for yourself that you can use when your journey gets difficult.

....

....

....

....

Be Curious! Be Real! Be Creative! Be Bold! Be YOU!!

I AM RESILIENT

YOU already have your own unique resiliency skills. Keep in mind that being resilient doesn't mean you don't feel anxious, triggered, depressed or insecure ever again. It does mean that when you've been through difficult experiences, especially as a child, you learn quickly how to adapt, cope and survive. Use this checklist to assess where YOUR resiliency skills are and work to continue to strengthen them. Add your own!

- ☐ I am resilient!
- ☐ I have already survived very difficult experiences, and I am capable and strong.
- ☐ I have been through more things than most teens my age and those things have given me knowledge and wisdom beyond my years.
- ☐ I am strong! I know how it feels to hurt and I can easily sense when others are hurting.
- ☐ I am the most knowledgeable person in the world about ME. NO ONE knows me better than I know myself.
- ☐ I believe in my own healing journey.
- ☐ I have people in my life who know me and care about me.
- ☐ I have a right to express all my hurt, sad, angry and upset feelings.
- ☐ I know there is only one me in this world, and I am in charge of creating my identity and the future I want for myself.
- ☐ I know my life has a purpose and even if it takes me a long time, I will discover and fight for the future I want for myself.
- ☐ I know my body, my heart and my mind are all precious. It's my job to surround myself with the things that help me heal on the inside.
- ☐ I can create positive, healthy relationships with people who love and care about me.
- ☐ I am valuable and worthy of living a positive and happy life.
- ☐ ?
- ☐ ?
- ☐ ?
- ☐ ?

Surviving can be turned into thriving!

SELF-MASTERY AND SELF-CONTROL

Guess what? YOU are already the hero in your own journey! Heroes have to go through challenges, dark times and difficult things on their way to finding out who they really are so they can learn how to use their superpowers! Write down what you've learned about YOURSELF on YOUR journey to both self-mastery and self-control. Include any future goals you may have to help YOU create the kind of life and relationships that are meaningful to YOU!

Self-mastery means to understand and become your 'real' and authentic self	• .... • .... • .... • .... • .... • .... • .... • .... • ....
Self-control means to manage your behaviors, impulses and emotions to achieve your goals	• .... • .... • .... • .... • .... • .... • .... • .... • ....

Self-discovery is a journey inward! Be true to YOURSELF!

THE PROS AND CONS OF CONTROL

There are both pros and cons to our controlling behaviors. Teens may use control to get their needs met or to protect themselves. Some teens may have a high need to control to avoid more pain and suffering, while others may use control to avoid feeling helpless or powerless. Write down the benefits (pros) and challenges (cons) in how YOU use controlling behaviors in your relationships.

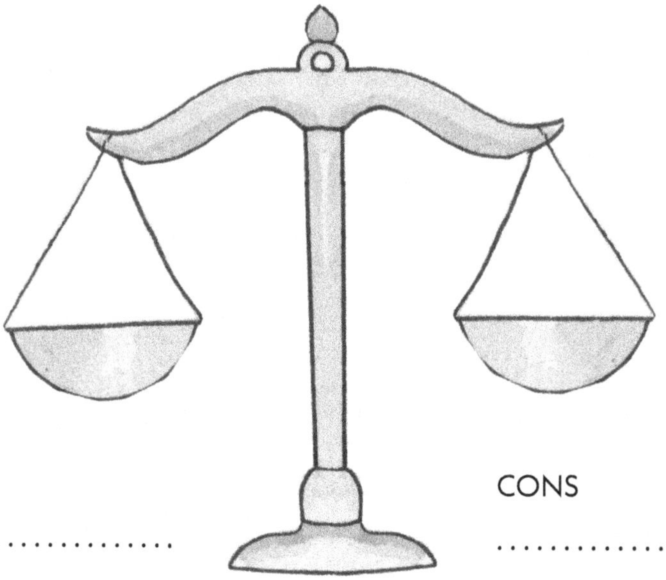

PROS

....
....
....
....
....
....
....

CONS

....
....
....
....
....
....
....

Change requires a leap of faith.

TO CONTROL OR NOT TO CONTROL!

Think about all of the things YOU CAN control: your beliefs, your attitude, your reactions to others, your thoughts, being honest, how you choose to spend your time, your decisions, how you respond to challenges. List all the things that you CAN control in your life.

Things I can control:

- ....
- ....
- ....
- ....
- ....
- ....
- ....
- ....
- ....

List all of the things YOU CANNOT control: someone else's opinions or their reactions or feelings, the past, what happens around you, how others view you, your genetics, someone else's decisions, the weather, your parent's mood, gossip, the news, and so on.

Things I cannot control:

- ....
- ....
- ....
- ....
- ....
- ....
- ....
- ....
- ....

my life is my story. It's my job to know and understand all the different parts so I can build a positive life for myself.

WHY I FIGHT FOR CONTROL!

From the moment we enter the world, we want control. We all have a desire to have power and control over our life and how it unfolds. Experiences like loss, trauma and abandonment can lead to feelings of hurt, pain and powerlessness. To counteract these feelings, we can get 'over-controlling' in our life and relationships. 'Under the surface' are the thoughts and feelings we might carry internally. Complete 'on the surface' with the actions and behaviors that might go with what's 'under the surface'.

Under the surface	On the surface
I'm anxious and worried all the time that something bad will happen again.	
I'm scared of getting too close. I don't deserve love and feel like I don't matter.	
I feel bad and blame myself for my losses or traumas.	
I feel helpless, as if I have NO control over my life and choices.	
I've been hurt a lot and no one sees my deep pain or suffering.	
I'm so angry all the time. I want a lot of control to avoid more losses.	

Understanding the NEED to control is the first step towards healing the emotions underneath the surface!

MY JOURNEY BELONGS TO ME!

The Seven Core Issues are 'normal' crisis issues, feelings and challenges that teens may experience during different parts of their life journey. Having these issues does NOT mean that there is anything wrong or 'damaged' or 'bad' about you. Rather, these are additional and expected emotions and challenges that come from the experience of adoption, kinship and foster care.

Teens may lose connections to both their maternal and paternal birth/first families; siblings, grandparents, aunts and uncles and cousins. They may lose cultural, racial and ethnic connections and/or their language of origin and even their country of origin. If they are in foster care or adopted as older children, they may also lose important friends, foster families, pets, schools, neighborhoods and familiar surroundings.

Being a teen is one of the most exciting times in your life. It's the stage of life where YOU get to figure out who you are, what you stand for, and what kind of life you want to live. For teens who are adopted or in foster or kinship care, you have had a lot of extra challenges in your life.

Reclaiming some of the power and control you lost and feeling empowered to search for parts of your identity and history is an important part of healing from the losses created by adoption and foster care. Exploring and healing from these issues will help you see just how resilient, strong and wise YOU really are!

YOUR journey belongs to you. YOU are the narrator of your story. Write well, edit often!

Use the Seven Core Issues grid to track your own journey.

- Write down the challenges, feelings and issues that you experienced as a 'child'.
- Next write down the challenges, feelings and issues that you experience now as a teen.
- Use colored pencils representing different emotions and color code your responses so you can capture the feelings, themes and emotions connected to those issues.
- As a teen, add your strengths and coping strategies for each of the issues.

Take your time completing the grid; these are heavy issues! Completing the grid will help you see and understand some of the growth and healing that has already occurred.

Seven Core Issues	My younger self	Me now, as a teen
Loss		
Rejection		
Shame/Guilt		
Grief		
Identity		
Intimacy		
Mastery/Control		

Exploring these issues within myself takes courage, strength and emotional space. I'm proud of myself for prioritizing my own growth and healing!

MY FORGIVING HEART

Forgiveness is an important part of mastery. Forgiving ourselves for the mistakes we've made is a BIG part of releasing old hurt and shame. When we make a mistake and cause pain or suffering to someone we love and care about, we can either beat ourselves up or we can make amends. When you have unhealed trauma or loss, it's easy to project that pain and hurt onto someone close to you. Making amends means taking responsibility for your words and actions that have created pain and hurt for others. Forgiveness is a learned skill that will help your relationships stay strong and healthy.

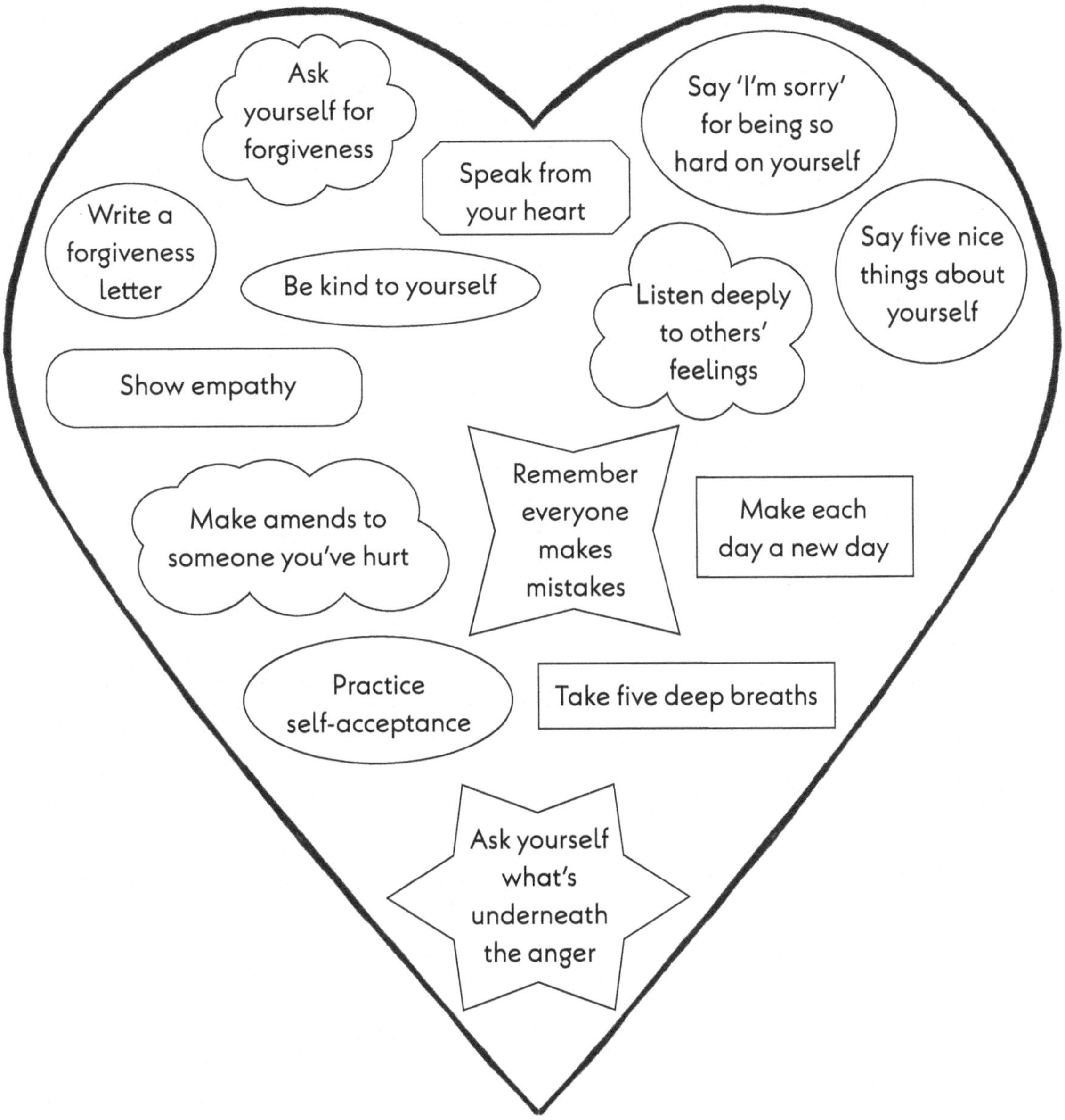

Learning to forgive MYSELF for the mistakes I made that came from my pain, loss or trauma is an important part of my healing journey!

MY HEALING MANDALA

Teens who have experienced loss, trauma and attachment disruptions may have not spent enough time in their childhood relaxing, playing, connecting, laughing and being joyful and silly. Let's make sure you find balance and learn to relax, laugh and heal. Complete your Healing Mandala with ALL the things that will support YOUR growth and healing in each of the mandala categories!

Living a meaningful life is all about me understanding me! This takes some internal work! I spend time each day taking good care of me!

MY GRATITUDE MAP

As you learn, grow and heal, it's easier to feel hopeful and optimistic about your life and future. Write down all the BIG and little things in YOUR life that YOU are grateful for on your Gratitude Map. Complete and put it up in your room so you see it every day to remind you of all the good things in YOUR life! Add more each day!

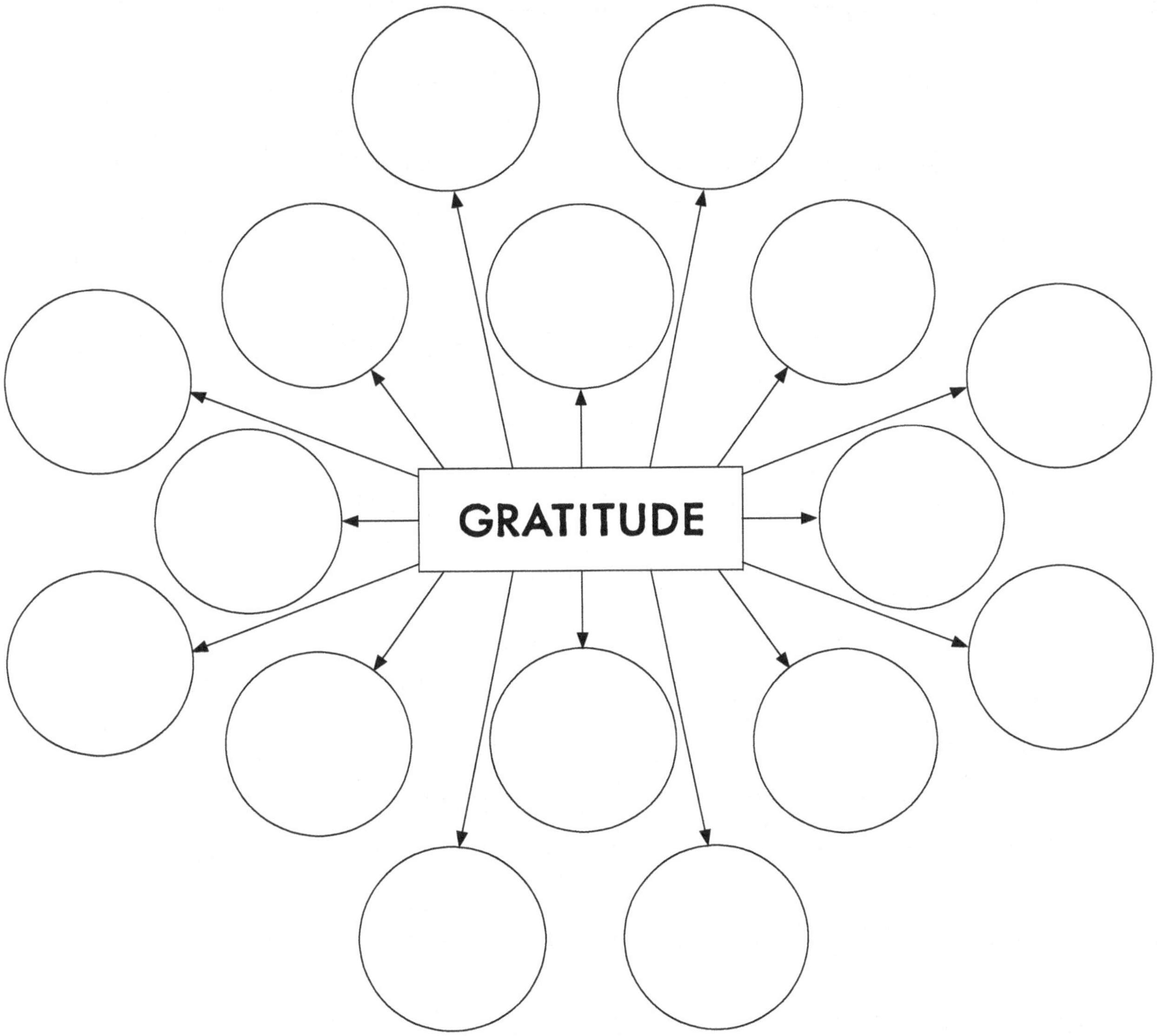

Use YOUR voice to speak YOUR truth.

FOUR STEPS TO MASTERY

This journey to mastery is not about achieving a goal or getting to a finish line. It's about the process of *learning* and *practicing* every day to be YOUR most authentic and real SELF. Being adopted or in foster/kinship care, you have experienced more challenges and losses than the average teen. Be patient with yourself as you learn more about your past and some of the missing pieces of YOUR story and history. Even if you have heard some of the facts of your story before, now that you're a teen, you have the BIG task of putting all those pieces together to build your identity and life path. Mastery is more like a marathon. Give yourself some time to explore and 'try on' different parts of your identity. Some things will 'fit well' and you'll want to hold on to those parts. Some things will 'not fit' and you can choose to 'let go' of those old patterns or beliefs—especially if they don't help you feel good and positive about YOURSELF! Remember to have as much compassion and empathy for yourself as you would have for a good friend or loved one.

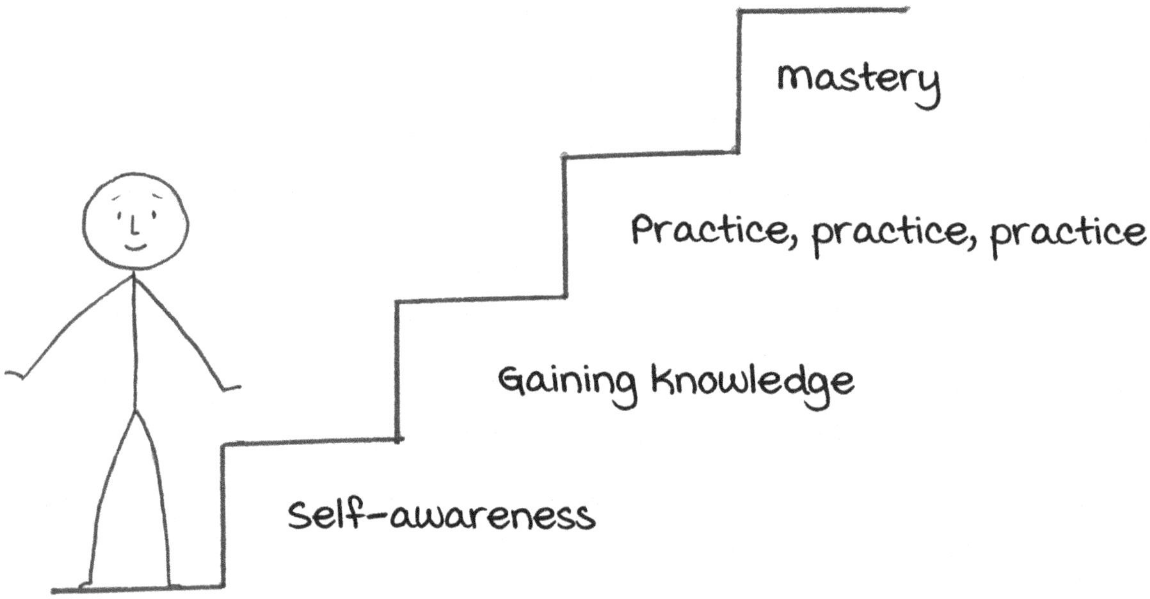

Steps to mastery:

1. **Self-awareness.** Examining who YOU are at your core so you can discover your purpose, needs and life goals; those parts of yourself that help you create a meaningful life. Write what you've learned about YOURSELF through this process of self-discovery.

   ....

   ....

   ....

....

....

2. **Gaining knowledge.** Using what you learned from step one, write down what knowledge, skills and which mentors can assist YOU on your path towards mastery. This is the 'learning' phase of mastery!

....

....

....

....

....

3. **Practice, practice, practice.** You must actively use the knowledge from step two and practice those skills in your life and relationships. Lots of practice is required, including making mistakes, getting feedback, learning something new, and practicing more. This is the 'doing' phase of mastery! What new skills did you practice today? How did it go?

....

....

....

....

....

4. **Mastery.** Remaining self-aware, practicing your new knowledge and skills with ease. This is the fun part of mastery. You feel strong, more confident and secure in YOUR authentic self! Write down a positive message to yourself. Congratulate yourself for all the hard work YOU put into your own healing journey!

....

....

....

....

....

Knowledge comes from learning; wisdom comes from experience!